American English

Personal Best

Student's Book

A1
Beginner

Series Editor
Jim Scrivener

Author
Graham Fruen

CONTENTS

		LANGUAGE			**SKILLS**	
		GRAMMAR	PRONUNCIATION	VOCABULARY		
1 My life		• the verb *be* (*I, you*) • the verb *be* (*he, she, it*) • the verb *be* (*we, you, they*)	• the alphabet • word stress • numbers	• greetings • classroom language • countries and nationalities • numbers 0–100 • jobs • adjectives (1)	**LISTENING** • a video introducing the *Learning Curve* team • listening for information about people • contractions	**WRITING** • filling out a form • capital letters **PERSONAL BEST** • a personal information form
Hello	p4					
1A	Where's she from?	p6				
1B	Welcome to *Learning Curve*!	p8				
1C	We are the champions	p10				
1D	What's your e-mail address?	p12				
2 People and things		• singular and plural nouns • *this, that, these, those* • possessive adjectives, *'s* for possession	• the /ɪ/ and /iy/ sounds • *'s*	• personal items • colors • family and friends	**READING** • an article about the Transportation for London Lost and Found Office • preparing to read • adjectives and nouns	**SPEAKING** • asking for information politely • telling the time **PERSONAL BEST** • asking for information at a movie theater or an airport
2A	The man with only 15 things	p14				
2B	Lost!	p16				
2C	My family	p18				
2D	What time is it?	p20				

1 and **2** — **REVIEW** and **PRACTICE**   p22

		LANGUAGE			**SKILLS**	
3 Food and drink		• simple present (*I, you, we, they*) • simple present (*he, she, it*)	• *do you* /dəyuw/ • *-s* and *-es* endings	• food and drink • days and times of day • common verbs (1)	**LISTENING** • A video about cafés around the world • listening for times and days • the /ə/ sound	**WRITING** • punctuation • linking words (*and, but*) **PERSONAL BEST** • a blog about a festival
3A	Food for athletes	p24				
3B	Tea or coffee?	p26				
3C	Chocolate for breakfast!	p28				
3D	A special meal	p30				
4 Daily life		• frequency adverbs • simple present: *wh-* questions	• sentence stress • question words	• daily routine verbs • transportation • adjectives (2)	**READING** • a text about New York's *citibikes* • finding specific information • *'s*: possession or contraction	**SPEAKING** • being polite in stores • grocery shopping **PERSONAL BEST** • buying things in a restaurant, café, or store
4A	Day and night	p32				
4B	My trip to work	p34				
4C	Where do you work?	p36				
4D	How can I help you?	p38				

3 and **4** — **REVIEW** and **PRACTICE**   p40

		LANGUAGE			**SKILLS**	
5 All about me		• *can* and *can't* • object pronouns	• *can* and *can't* • the /h/ sound	• common verbs (2) • electronic devices • activities	**LISTENING** • a video about the importance of electronic devices • listening for specific information • sentence stress	**WRITING** • describing yourself • *because* **PERSONAL BEST** • an online profile
5A	When can you start?	p42				
5B	I can't live without my phone	p44				
5C	I love it!	p46				
5D	My profile	p48				

Language App, unit-by-unit grammar and vocabulary games

CONTENTS

		LANGUAGE			SKILLS	
		GRAMMAR	PRONUNCIATION	VOCABULARY		
6 Places		■ *there is/are* ■ prepositions of place	■ linking consonants and vowels ■ sentence stress	■ places in a town ■ parts of the body ■ rooms and furniture	READING ■ an article about art in public spaces ■ reading in detail ■ giving opinions	SPEAKING ■ checking information ■ asking for and giving directions **PERSONAL BEST** ■ a conversation asking for and giving directions
6A	City or town? p50					
6B	City art p52					
6C	An unusual home p54					
6D	Is there a post office near here? p56					

5 and **6** REVIEW and PRACTICE p58

		LANGUAGE			SKILLS	
7 All in the past		■ simple past: *be* ■ simple past: regular verbs	■ *was/were* ■ *-ed* endings	■ celebrities ■ months and ordinals ■ time expressions	LISTENING ■ a video about Shakespeare and the theater ■ listening for dates ■ linking consonants and vowels	WRITING ■ writing informal e-mails ■ sequencers **PERSONAL BEST** ■ an e-mail about an interesting weekend
7A	When they were young p60					
7B	I was there in July p62					
7C	Famous decades p64					
7D	A weekend away p66					

		LANGUAGE			SKILLS	
8 Travel		■ simple past: irregular verbs ■ *there was/were*	■ irregular simple past verbs ■ sentence stress	■ travel verbs ■ weather and seasons ■ nature	READING ■ posts about an unusual trip on a travel website ■ understanding the main idea ■ modifiers	SPEAKING ■ starting and ending a phone call at work ■ buying a ticket **PERSONAL BEST** ■ a phone call buying a ticket
8A	Incredible trips p68					
8B	Crazy weather! p70					
8C	Then and now p72					
8D	A trip to Canada p74					

7 and **8** REVIEW and PRACTICE p76

		LANGUAGE			SKILLS	
9 Shopping		■ present continuous ■ *how often* + frequency expressions	■ *-ing* endings ■ sentence stress	■ clothes ■ feelings ■ shopping	LISTENING ■ a video about how our clothes affect how we feel ■ identifying key points ■ filler words	WRITING ■ describing a photo ■ describing position **PERSONAL BEST** ■ an e-mail describing a photo
9A	Street style p78					
9B	How do you feel? p80					
9C	Love it or hate it? p82					
9D	Garage sale p84					

		LANGUAGE			SKILLS	
10 Time out		■ present continuous for future plans ■ question review	■ sentence stress ■ intonation in questions	■ free-time activities ■ types of music and movies ■ sports and games	READING ■ a listings page from an entertainment website ■ scanning for information ■ the imperative	SPEAKING ■ showing interest ■ asking about a tourist attraction **PERSONAL BEST** ■ a conversation about a tourist attraction
10A	What are you doing on the weekend? p86					
10B	What's on? p88					
10C	Royal hobbies p90					
10D	Where are we going now? p92					

9 and **10** REVIEW and PRACTICE p94

Grammar practice p96　　Vocabulary practice p106　　Communication practice p134　　Irregular verbs p151

Language App, unit-by-unit grammar and vocabulary games

UNIT 1 My life

LANGUAGE the verb *be* (*I, you*) ■ greetings ■ classroom language

Hello

1 ▶ 1.1 Read and listen. Match conversations 1–3 with pictures a–c.

1 **Wendy** Good morning. Are you Emma, the new teacher?
  Emma Yes, I am.
  Wendy I'm Wendy. Nice to meet you. You're in Class 3.
  Emma Thanks, Wendy. See you later.

2 **Emma** Hello, I'm Emma. What's your name?
  Kiko Hi, my name's Kiko.
  Emma Nice to meet you, Kiko.
  Kiko Are you a student here?
  Emma No, I'm not. I'm your teacher!

3 **Kiko** Emma, this is my friend, Misha.
  Emma Hello. Hmm, you're not in Class 3, Misha.
  Misha No, I'm in Class 4, and I'm late! Goodbye!
  Emma Bye, Misha!

2 Put the words from the conversations in the correct columns. Can you add any other words?

Bye Good morning Hi See you later	Hello	Goodbye

3 A ▶ 1.2 Listen and repeat the highlighted phrases from the conversations in exercise 1. How do you say them in your language?

B Practice the conversations from exercise 1 in groups of four.

4 A Complete the sentences with the words in the box. Then check your answers in the conversations.

're   'm   'm not   're not   Are

1 I _____ Wendy.
2 You _____ in Class 3.
3 _____ you a student here?
4 No, I _____ .
5 You _____ in Class 3, Misha.

B ▶ 1.3 Listen and repeat the contractions in **bold**. Then read the Grammar box.

1 I am = **I'm**   2 You are = **You're**   3 You are not = **You're not**

Grammar   the verb *be* (*I, you*)

Affirmative:
I'm Wendy.
You're in Class 4.

Negative:
You're not in Class 3.
I'm not a student.

Questions and short answers:
Are you a teacher?
Yes, *I am*.   No, *I'm not*.

Go to Grammar practice: the verb *be* (*I, you*), page 96

the verb *be* (*I*, *you*) ■ greetings ■ classroom language   LANGUAGE   **Hello**

5 **A** ▶ 1.5 Complete the conversation. Listen and check.

Kiko Hello. What's ¹_____ name?
Eleni ²_____ name's Eleni.
Kiko Nice to ³_____ you, Eleni. I ⁴_____ Kiko.
Eleni Nice to meet you, Kiko. ⁵_____ you a student here?
Kiko ⁶ Yes, I _____ .

B In pairs, practice the conversation using your names.

6 Introduce yourself and your partner to another pair.
  A *Hello, I'm Caro. This is Pablo.*
  B *Nice to meet you. My name's Malika, and this is Petra.*

7 ▶ 1.6 Read the phrases and write *Teacher* or *Student*. Listen and check.

1 _____ Open your books.
2 _____ Excuse me, what does "late" mean?
3 _____ I'm sorry, I don't understand.
4 _____ Listen and repeat.
5 _____ How do you say "buenos días" in English?
6 _____ Work in pairs.

Go to **Vocabulary practice:** classroom language, page 106

8 ▶ 1.8 **Pronunciation:** the alphabet Listen and repeat the sounds, words, and letters.

/ey/	/iy/	/e/	/ay/	/ow/	/uw/	/ɑ/
late	meet	yes	my	no	you	pasta
Aa Hh Jj Kk	Bb Cc Dd Ee Gg Pp Tt Vv Zz	Ff Ll Mm Nn Ss Xx	Ii Yy	Oo	Qq Uu Ww	Rr

9 ▶ 1.9 Listen to the conversations. Write the names of the students.

Class 3
Student names:
1 _____
2 _____
3 _____

ABC
ABC School of English

Go to **Communication practice:** Student A page 134, Student B page 142

10 Introduce yourself to five students. Ask the questions and write the answers.

What's your name?   How do you spell that?

Personal Best Write a conversation between a teacher and a new student.

5

1 LANGUAGE
the verb *be* (*he, she, it*) ■ countries and nationalities ■ numbers 0–10

1A Where's she from?

1 A In pairs, match the flags with the countries.

A *What's flag "a"?* B *I think it's Mexico.*

c   d   e   f   g   h

| 1 Argentina ____ | 3 China ____ | 5 Spain ____ | 7 the UK ____ |
| 2 Brazil ____ | 4 Mexico ____ | 6 Turkey ____ | 8 the U.S. ____ |

B ▶ 1.10 Listen, check, and repeat.

2 A ▶ 1.11 Listen to the conversation. Repeat it in pairs.

A Where are you from? **A** Where's Salta?
B I'm from Salta. **B** It's in Argentina.

B In pairs, practice the conversation using the cities and countries.

Toledo / Spain   Izmir / Turkey   Harbin / China   York / the UK

I'm from the UK.
I'm British.

3 Look at the picture. Match the countries from exercise 1 with the nationalities.

1 British	_the UK_	4 American	_____	7 Turkish	_____
2 Spanish	_____	5 Argentinian	_____	8 Brazilian	_____
3 Mexican	_____	6 Chinese	_____		

Go to Vocabulary practice: countries and nationalities, page 107

4 ▶ 1.13 Do the quiz in pairs. Listen and check.

THE C🌐UNTRIES QUIZ

1 What nationality is Meghan Markle?
a She's British.
b She's American.

5 Which sentence is correct?
a Sydney is the capital of Australia.
b Sydney's not the capital of Australia.

2 Where is Mount Fuji?
a It's in China.
b It's in Japan.

6 Is *ceviche* Mexican or Peruvian?
a It's Mexican.
b It's Peruvian.

3 Is this elephant from India or Africa?
a It's from India.
b It's from Africa.

7 Where is the Bosphorus?
a It's in Turkey.
b It's in Russia.

4 Is Selena Gómez Russian?
a Yes, she is.
b No, she's not.

8 What nationality is Paulo Coelho?
a He's Italian.
b He's Brazilian.

the verb *be* (*he*, *she*, *it*) ■ countries and nationalities ■ numbers 0–10   **LANGUAGE 1A**

5 A Match the pronouns *he*, *she*, and *it* with the people and things.
1 he a Selena Gómez
2 she b ceviche
3 it c Paulo Coelho

B Check (✓) the form of the verb *be* that we use with *he*, *she*, and *it*. Then read the Grammar box.
1 am ☐ 2 is ☐ 3 are ☐

Grammar — the verb *be* (*he*, *she*, *it*)

Affirmative:
He's Japanese.
She's from Mexico.

Negative:
Barcelona **isn't** the capital of Spain.
She**'s not** Australian. / She **isn't** Australian.

Questions and short answers:
Is it from India?
Yes, it **is**.   No, it**'s not**. / No, it **isn't**.

Go to Grammar practice: the verb *be* (*he*, *she*, *it*), page 96

6 A ▶ 1.15 **Pronunciation:** word stress Listen and repeat the words. Pay attention to the underlined stressed syllables.

Ja<u>pan</u>   Japa<u>nese</u>   <u>Mex</u>ico   <u>Mex</u>ican   <u>It</u>aly   <u>It</u>alian   <u>Tur</u>key   <u>Tur</u>kish

B ▶ 1.16 <u>Underline</u> the stress in the countries and nationalities. Then listen, check, and repeat.
1 I'm Brazilian. 2 She's from Germany. 3 It's Chinese. 4 Is he from Argentina?

7 In pairs, ask and answer the question *Where's … from?* about the people and things.
A *Where's Zara from?*   **B** *Is it Italian?*
A *No, it's not. It's Spanish.*

 Zara  Ryan Gosling  Mercedes  Thalía  Neymar  Chow mein

8 A ▶ 1.17 Listen and repeat the numbers.

zero/oh   one   two   three   four   five   six   seven   eight   nine   ten

B ▶ 1.18 What are the country calling codes? Listen and write the answers.
1 China + _____
2 Colombia + _____
3 India + _____
4 Mexico + _____
5 Spain + _____
6 Turkey + _____

Go to Communication practice: Student A page 134, Student B page 142

9 A In pairs, write six more quiz questions about countries and nationalities.
B Work with another pair. Ask and answer your quiz questions.
A *What is the capital of Peru? a) It's Lima. b) It's Bogotá.*
B *It's not Bogotá – that's in Colombia. I think it's Lima.*
A *That's right! Your turn.*

Personal Best Write six sentences about people and things you like. Say where they are from.

7

1 SKILLS LISTENING listening for information about people ■ contractions ■ jobs

1B Welcome to *Learning Curve*!

1 Match the jobs in the box with pictures a–f.

doctor engineer office worker police officer taxi driver waiter

Go to Vocabulary practice: jobs, page 108

2 A 1.20 Look at the picture. Listen and complete the conversation.

A What's my job?
B Are you an ¹_____ ?
A No, I'm not. Try again!
B Are you a ²_____ ?
A Yes, I am.

B In pairs, play "What's my job?"

3 1.21 Watch or listen to the start of a webshow called *Learning Curve*. Match the cities with the people.

1 New York   a Simon, Kate, Marina
2 London   b Ethan, Penny, Mohammed, Marc

Skill listening for information about people

We often listen to information about people.
- Don't worry if you don't understand everything the speakers say.
- Read the questions and think about the information you need to listen for: name, job, nationality, etc.
- Listen for the verb *be*: *I'm … / He's … / She's …* etc.

4 1.21 Read the Skill box. Watch or listen again, and choose the correct information about the people.

Simon Collins
Nationality: British
Job: ¹ *TV host / receptionist*

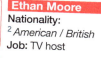
Ethan Moore
Nationality: ² *American / British*
Job: TV host

Penny Abernathy
Nationality: English and ³ *Italian / Argentinian*
Job: TV host

Marina Ivanova
Nationality: Russian
Job: ⁴ *receptionist / teacher*

Mohammed Bensallem
Nationality: American
Job: ⁵ *TV host / office worker*

Marc Kim
Nationality: American
Job: ⁶ *doctor / IT specialist*

Kate McRea
Nationality: ⁷ *American / Argentinian*
Job: TV host

listening for information about people ■ contractions ■ jobs   LISTENING   SKILLS   1B

5 ▶ 1.22 Watch or listen to the rest of the show. Who's not in London now? Where is he/she?

Viktor

Sarah

Pedro

6 ▶ 1.22 Watch or listen again. Complete the information with countries and jobs.
1 Viktor: from: _____ job: _____ and _____
2 Sarah: from: _____ job: _____
3 Pedro: from: _____ job: _____

7 A In pairs, ask and answer the questions about the three people.
(Where is … from?) (What's his/her job?)

B In pairs, ask and answer the questions about you.
(Where are you from?) (What's your job?)

8 ▶ 1.23 Listen and read what Kate says. How does she say the contractions in **bold**? What do they mean?

Hi, **I'm** Kate from *Learning Curve*. **What's** your name?

Listening builder | contractions

In English, we often use contractions, especially when we speak.
I'm from the United States. = *I am* from the United States.
She's not a student. = *She is* not a student.
What's your job? = *What is* your job?

9 ▶ 1.24 Read the Listening builder. Listen and write the contractions.
1 _____ Spanish.   3 He _____ a doctor.   5 _____ an engineer.
2 _____ your name?   4 _____ from Japan.   6 The _____ here.

10 ▶ 1.25 In pairs, look at the pictures of Jia and Luis. Guess the information about the people. Listen to the conversations and check.

(job?) (nationality?) (Where now?)

11 Write the names of three friends or members of your family. In pairs, ask and answer questions about them.

A *Where's Saanvi from?*   B *She's from Nagpur.*
A *What's her job?*   B *She's an IT worker.*
A *Where is she now?*   B *She's in Mumbai.*

Jia

Luis

Personal Best Choose five classmates and write their jobs, e.g., *Carla's a teacher.*

9

1 LANGUAGE

the verb *be* (*we, you, they*) ■ numbers 11–100 ■ adjectives (1)

1C We are the champions

1 A Write the numbers in the box in the correct order.

sixteen thirteen fourteen seventeen twelve twenty ~~eleven~~ fifteen nineteen eighteen

eleven, _____

B Look at the pictures and read the numbers. Check (✓) the numbers that are correct.

1 twenty-three ☐   2 fifty-four ☐   3 eighty-six ☐   4 sixty-eight ☐   5 one hundred ☐   6 thirty ☐

Go to Vocabulary practice: numbers 0–100, page 111

2 A In pairs, ask and answer the question *How old is …?* for the people in the picture.

A *How old is Kyle?*   **B** *I think he's 40.*

B ▶ 1.27   Listen and write the ages.

Kyle _____   Martin _____   Lorna _____

Kyle   Martin   Lorna

3 A Look at the picture. What do you know about the rock band Queen? Do you know any songs or the names of the band members?

B Read the introduction to the interview. What is the name of the band?

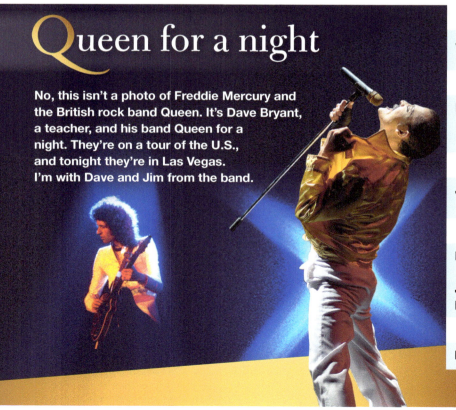

Queen for a night

No, this isn't a photo of Freddie Mercury and the British rock band Queen. It's Dave Bryant, a teacher, and his band Queen for a night. They're on a tour of the U.S., and tonight they're in Las Vegas. I'm with Dave and Jim from the band.

So Jim, are you all teachers?

Jim   No, we're not. I'm an engineer, and Ed and Mick are doctors.

And where are you from?

Dave   I'm from New York, Jim and Ed are from Boston, and Mick's from Atlantic City. We're old friends from college.

How's the tour going?

Jim   It's good, but it's hard. It's a big tour – fourteen cities – and we're not so young now!

Really? How old are you?

Dave   Mick and I are forty-seven. And you and Ed are fifty …

Jim   I'm not fifty! Ed's fifty … I'm forty-nine.

Dave   Oh yeah. Sorry, Jim!

And what's your favorite Queen song?

Dave   That's easy! It's *We Are the Champions*!

the verb *be* (*we*, *you*, *they*) ■ numbers 11–100 ■ adjectives (1) **LANGUAGE 1C**

4 ▶ 1.28 Read and listen to the interview. Complete the information about the band.

	Dave	Jim	Ed	Mick
job				
city				
age				

5 A Read the sentences from the interview. Match the people in **bold** with the pronouns *we*, *you*, and *they*.

1 **Mick and I** are forty-seven. ____   2 **Jim and Ed** are from Boston. ____   3 And **you and Ed** are fifty. ____

B Check (✓) the form of the verb *be* we use when we talk about more than one person. Then read the Grammar box.

a am / am not ☐   b is / is not ☐   c are / are not ☐

📖 **Grammar**   the verb *be* (*we*, *you*, *they*)

Affirmative:
We**'re** old friends.
They**'re** on a tour of the U.S.

Negative:
We**'re not** young.
They**'re not** the rock band Queen.

Questions and short answers:
Are you all teachers?
Yes, we **are**.   No, we**'re not**.

Go to Grammar practice: the verb *be* (*we*, *you*, *they*), page 96

6 A ▶ 1.30 **Pronunciation: numbers** Listen and repeat the numbers. Pay attention to how the stress changes.

1 a thir**teen**   b **thir**ty   2 a four**teen**   b **for**ty   3 a fif**teen**   b **fif**ty

B ▶ 1.31 Listen and check (✓) the numbers you hear. Listen again and repeat.

1 a He's not 16. ☐   b He's not 60. ☐   3 a We're not 17. ☐   b We're not 70. ☐
2 a She's 18. ☐   b She's 80. ☐   4 a They're 19. ☐   b They're 90. ☐

Go to Communication practice: Student A page 134, Student B page 142

7 Match adjectives 1–4 from the interview with their opposites in the box.

> bad   small   old   difficult

1 young _____   2 good _____   3 big _____   4 easy _____

Go to Vocabulary practice: adjectives (1), page 109

8 Describe the pictures in pairs. Use affirmative and negative forms.

Picture a: They're big. They're not small.

9 A In small groups, imagine you are in a band and complete the chart.

The name of the band	Your names	Your ages	Nationalities

B Work with another group. Interview each other about your bands.

What's the name of your band?   What are your names?   How old are you?   Where are you from?

Personal Best   Write a short paragraph about a band you like.

11

1 SKILLS WRITING filling out a form ■ capital letters

1D What's your e-mail address?

1 Match the places in the box with pictures a–c.

> hotel   car rental office   gym

2 A Look at the form. Match it with one of the pictures in exercise 1.

B ▶ 1.33 Listen to the conversation. Which piece of information in the form is **incorrect**?

Customer Information — CARS-4-U

Title	MR. ☐ MS. ✓ MRS. ☐
Last name	Martín
First name(s)	Luisa
Nationality	Mexican
Date of birth	06/17/1980
Street address	Calle de la Paz, 65, Puebla, Mexico
Zip code	72160
e-mail address	luisa.martin@mymail.com
Phone number	52-222-266-5647

 Skill filling out a form

When you fill out a form, read all the instructions and sections carefully.
- Use the correct *title*. *Mr.* = a man, *Ms.* = a woman (married or unmarried), *Mrs.* = a married woman.
- Your *last name* is your family name.
- Write your *date of birth* in numbers: the month/the day/the year: *09/13/1995*.
- For e-mail addresses: @ = "at" and .com = "dot com."

3 Read the Skill box. Match sections 1–9 with information a–i.

1 zip code
2 date of birth
3 street address
4 last name
5 first name
6 e-mail address
7 title
8 phone number
9 nationality

a Taylor
b 17401
c Mr.
d c.taylor@candb.com
e 717-322-5623
f 11/23/1988
g American
h Carl
i 3927 Stout Street, York, PA

12

filling out a form ■ capital letters **WRITING** **SKILLS** **1D**

4 In pairs, ask and answer questions about you, using the information in exercise 3.
A *What's your last name?* B *It's Taylor.*
A *How do you spell that?* B *It's T-A-Y-L-O-R.*

5 Look at answers a–i in exercise 3. Check (✓) the information with capital letters.
1 first name ☐ 3 e-mail address ☐ 5 street ☐
2 last name ☐ 4 nationality ☐ 6 city ☐

Text builder — capital letters

In English, we use capital letters (*A*, *B*, *C*, *D*, etc.) for the following:
- the first word in a sentence: *What's your name?*
- the personal pronoun *I*: *Hello, I'm Robert.*
- the names of people and places: *Emma is from Boston.*
- countries, nationalities, and languages: *We're from China. We're Chinese.*

6 A Read the Text builder. Find one **incorrect** capital letter in each sentence.
1 My friend Lena is American. She's From Florida.
2 Hello, I'm Antonio. I'm a new Student.
3 Our street Address is 8927 North Winery Ave, Austin, TX 73301.
4 This is Mesut. He's from Turkey and he's Twenty-one.

B Rewrite the sentences with capital letters.
1 what's his job? is he a doctor? _____
2 my street address is 11004 spruce run, san diego, ca 92131. _____
3 they aren't from germany. they're from poland. _____
4 i'm your new english teacher. my name's jack. _____

7 A PREPARE Look at the form. Be sure that you understand all the information you need to write.

B PRACTICE Fill out your form. Remember to use capital letters correctly.

C PERSONAL BEST Exchange forms with a partner. Is it clear and easy to read? Are the capital letters correct?

Personal Best Design a form for a gym. Fill it out with information about a family member.

UNIT 2 People and things

LANGUAGE singular and plural nouns ■ *this*, *that*, *these*, *those* ■ personal items

2A The man with only 15 things

1 ▶ 2.1 In pairs, match the words in the box with objects a–f. Listen and check.

| a book   a purse   keys   a watch   an umbrella   a camera |

 a
 b
 c
 d
 e
 f

Go to Vocabulary practice: personal items, page 110

2 Look at exercise 1 and answer the questions. Then read the Grammar box.

1 Which noun do we use with *an*? _____
2 Which noun is plural? _____

 Grammar   singular and plural nouns

Singular nouns: *a key*   *an umbrella*   *a watch*
Plural nouns: *keys*   *umbrellas*   *watches*

Go to Grammar practice: singular and plural nouns, page 97

3 **A** Imagine you live with only 15 things. What are your 15 things?
  B Read the text. Are your 15 things the same as Andrew's?

15 countries with 15 things

This is Andrew Hyde, and that's his book: *15 countries with 15 things*. Andrew is from Colorado in the U.S., and he's a writer and traveler. And it's true – he's a man with only 15 things!

THESE ARE HIS 15 THINGS:

1 ___ backpack	6 ___ wallet	13 ___ shoes
2 ___ smartphone	7 ___ jacket	14 ___ towel
3 ___ camera	8 ___ pants	15 ___ toiletry bag
4 ___ iPad	9 & 10 ___ shirts	
5 ___ sunglasses	11 & 12 ___ shorts	

Andrew is back in the U.S. now, but is he happy with just those 15 things? Yes, he says. Life is easy without a lot of things.

14

singular and plural nouns ■ *this*, *that*, *these*, *those* ■ personal items   **LANGUAGE 2A**

4 Look at the list of Andrew's things again. Write *a* or *an* for singular nouns, and – for plural nouns.

5 Complete the sentences from the text with the pronouns in the box. Which words do we use with singular nouns? Which ones with plural nouns? Then read the Grammar box.

that   those   this   these

1 _____ is Andrew Hyde.
2 _____'s his book.
3 _____ are his 15 things.
4 Is he happy with just _____ 15 things?

Grammar *this*, *that*, *these*, *those*

Things that are near us:
This is my purse.
These are my keys.

Things that aren't near us:
That's my car.
Those are my friends.

Go to Grammar practice: *this, that, these, those*, page 97

6 A ▶ 2.5 **Pronunciation:** the /ɪ/ and /iy/ sounds Listen and repeat the sounds and words.

/ɪ/   this   it   is   six
/iy/   these   he   three keys

B ▶ 2.6 In pairs, say the sentences. Listen, check, and repeat.

1 This is my city.
2 These are my keys.
3 Is that tree Japanese?
4 She's six and he's three.

Go to Communication practice: Students A and B page 135

7 Choose the correct words to complete the text.

What's in your bag?

Maria Clara, office worker, Rio de Janeiro

¹ *This / These* is my purse and ² *this / these* are my things. This ³ *is / are* my book. It's in English! ⁴ *These / That* are my keys. ⁵ *This / These* key is for my house and ⁶ *that / those* key is for my car. ⁷ *This is / That's* my car over there – it's ⁸ *a / an* sports car! What's this? It's ⁹ *a / an* umbrella. It's very small! And the last thing? These are ¹⁰ *a / –* sunglasses!

8 A ▶ 2.7 Listen and match conversations 1–3 with pictures a–c.

B ▶ 2.7 Complete the phrases from the conversations with *this*, *that*, *these*, and *those*. Listen again and check.

1 Jack   What's _____?
2 Woman   Jorge, who's _____ over there?
3 Man   Hi, Karen. What are _____?

Helen   _____ is my purse.
Jorge   _____'s Sergio.
Karen   _____ are my cameras.

9 Put some things from your purse or backpack on the desk. In pairs, ask and answer questions about the things.

A *What's that?*   **B** *This is a book. It's in Spanish.*   **A** *And what are those?*   **B** *These are my keys.*

Personal Best   Write about the things in your purse or backpack, as in exercise 7.

2 SKILLS READING preparing to read ■ adjectives and nouns ■ colors

2B Lost!

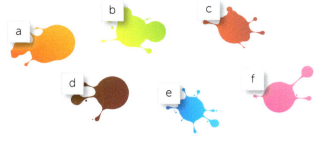

1 A Match the words in the box with the colors.

> blue brown green orange pink red

Go to Vocabulary practice: colors, page 110

B In pairs, point to items in the classroom. Ask and answer *What color is that/are those...?*

A *What color are those books?*   **B** *They're orange.*

Skill preparing to read

Before you read a text, look at other information to help you prepare.
- Think about the style of the text. Is it from a magazine, a website, a letter?
- Look at the pictures. What people, places, and things can you see?
- Read the title. What does it mean?

2 A Read the Skill box. What do you think the text on page 17 is about? Check (✓) a, b, or c.
a lost tourists in London ☐   b transportation in London ☐   c lost items in London ☐

B Read the text quickly and check your answer.

3 Read the text again. Are the sentences true (T) or false (F)?
1 The Lost and Found Office is in London. ____
2 The items are all from buses. ____
3 Tim Carlisle is a tour guide every day. ____
4 The laptop is new. ____
5 All the musical instruments are expensive. ____
6 The $15,000 is in the office now. ____

4 Complete the sentences with the words in the box. Check your answers in the text.

> expensive violin guitars cheap

1 These _____ are _____ .   2 That's an _____ _____ .

Text builder adjectives and nouns

adjective + noun: $15,000 in a **brown envelope**.
noun + be + adjective: This **laptop is new**.

Look! Adjectives don't change with plural nouns: *It's an **expensive instrument**. They're **expensive instruments**.*

5 Read the Text builder. Put the words in order to make sentences.
1 good it's a camera   _____
2 sunglasses they're expensive   _____
3 green purse the is   _____
4 are the brown wallets   _____
5 fast a it's car   _____

6 A ▶ 2.9 Read and listen to the conversation in a Lost and Found Office.

B In pairs, change the highlighted words and make a new conversation.

A Hello, can I help you?
B Do you have my wallet? It's a small, black wallet. It's expensive.
A Hold on. Is this your wallet?
B Yes, that's it!

16

preparing to read ■ adjectives and nouns ■ colors   READING   SKILLS   2B

Lost in London

22,000 cell phones, 12,000 credit cards, a green "Incredible Hulk" toy, $15,000 in a brown envelope …

These are some of the things in the Transportation for London Lost and Found Office. Every year, 300,000 items are lost on buses, trains, and taxis in the city. I'm at the office in central London, and with me is Tim Carlisle. Tim is an employee here, but today he's my tour guide.

"Look at all these things – wallets, glasses, purses, backpacks, shoes, cell phones – they're all here," Tim tells me. "Look at this laptop – it's new."

In a different part of the office are musical instruments. "These guitars are cheap, but that's an expensive violin," he says.

"What's over there?" I ask.

"Those are umbrellas. Big umbrellas, small umbrellas, blue umbrellas, pink umbrellas …"

"And what about the envelope with $15,000?" I ask. "Is it still here?"

"No," Tim says. "An old man collected it last month. He's 80 years old and he doesn't like banks!"

And that's the end of my tour. It's time for me to go. Now, where's my phone?

Personal Best   Write a conversation in a Lost and Found Office.

2 LANGUAGE

possessive adjectives, 's for possession ■ family and friends

2C My family

1 Match the people in the box with pictures a–d.

husband and wife   mother and son   father and daughter   brother and sister

2 Put the words from exercise 1 in the correct columns.

Male ♂	Female ♀
brother	sister

Go to Vocabulary practice: family and friends, page 111

3 A Discuss the questions in pairs.
1 Are you from a big family or a small family?
2 Do you live with your family?
3 Does anyone in your family live in a different city or country?

B Read the text quickly. What is Laura's family situation? Is she sad about it?

Long-distance families

Are you part of a "long-distance" family? Are your brothers or sisters in a different city or country? Are you a long way from your parents or children? Tell us your stories.

Laura Wickham

Hi! My name's Laura. My husband Seamus and I are long-distance parents! We live in Cork in Ireland. Our daughter Amy is 30 years old, and she's in Australia. Our son Conor is 26 years old, and he's in the U.S. Amy and Conor are a long distance from us, but their lives are very interesting. Amy's an IT worker in Perth. Her husband Pete is from there. He's an engineer. Conor's a surfing teacher in Los Angeles. He loves California and its beautiful beaches, so it's his dream job! Conor's girlfriend Nicole is a Hollywood actor … well, that's her dream. Right now, she's a waitress.
We're on Skype a lot with our children, but it's difficult with the time differences. Am I sad that they're so far away? Sometimes, but the important thing is that they're happy.

4 Read the text again. Match the information with the people.

1 This person is 30 years old.   a Seamus
2 This person is a waitress.   b Amy
3 This person lives in Cork.   c Pete
4 This person is a surfing teacher.   d Conor
5 This person is Australian.   e Nicole

possessive adjectives, 's for possession ■ family and friends   LANGUAGE **2C**

5 Complete the sentences from the text with the words in the box.

> our   my   her   its   his   their

1 _____ name's Laura.
2 _____ son Conor is 26 years old.
3 _____ lives are very interesting.
4 _____ husband Pete is from there.
5 He loves California and _____ beautiful beaches.
6 It's _____ dream job!

6 A Choose the correct option to complete the sentence from the text.

Conor's / Pete's / Seamus's girlfriend Nicole is a Hollywood actor.

B What ending do we add to names and nouns to show possession? Read the Grammar box.

📖 Grammar   possessive adjectives, 's for possession

Possessive adjectives:

I	my:	I'm a teacher. **My** name's Karen.
you	your:	Are you OK? **Your** phone's broken.
he	his:	He's a tour guide. **His** job's interesting.
she	her:	She's Chinese, but **her** husband's British.
it	its:	Sydney's a great city. **Its** beaches are beautiful.
we	our:	We're in Class 3, and **our** teacher's very good!
they	their:	Jo and Ben aren't here. They're in **their** car.

's for possession:

Kim's mother is from Germany.
Is this **Amy's** book?
My **son's** new phone is expensive.

Go to Grammar practice: possessive adjectives, 's for possession, page 97

7 A ▶ 2.12 **Pronunciation:** 's Listen and repeat. Pay attention to the 's sound.

son's   daughter's   Amy's   Conor's   my husband's   my sister's

B ▶ 2.13 In pairs, say the sentences. Then listen, check, and repeat.

1 My husband's name is Felipe.
2 Our son's girlfriend is French.
3 My wife's parents are from Canada.
4 Sara's brother's girlfriend is a doctor.

Go to Communication practice: Student A page 135, Student B page 143

8 ▶ 2.14 Look at the people. In pairs, guess their relationship. Listen and check.

A *I think Jim is Tom Hanks's son.*   **B** *Yes, or maybe he's his brother.*

Tom Hanks

Victoria Beckham

Will Smith

Shakira

Andy Murray

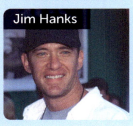
Jim Hanks

Louise Adams

Jaden Smith

Gerard Piqué

Judy Murray

9 Choose five people in your family and write down their names. In pairs, ask and answer questions about the people.

A *Who is Azra?*   **B** *She's my brother's wife.*

> Who is he/she?   How old is he/she?   What is his/her job?

Personal Best   Write a description of your family.

2 SKILLS SPEAKING asking for information politely ■ telling the time

2D What time is it?

1 A ▶ 2.15 In pairs, match the times in the box with the clocks. Listen and check.

> five o'clock   eight ten   quarter after/past ten   six thirty   eleven forty-five   three fifty-five

1 _____   2 _____   3 _____   4 _____   5 _____   6 _____

B ▶ 2.16 Complete the times. Listen, check, and repeat.

1 It's eleven _____ .   2 It's _____ three.   3 It's twelve _____ .   4 It's eight _____ .

2 A ▶ 2.17 Watch or listen to the start of *Learning Curve*. Choose the correct options to complete the sentences.

1 Kate is _____ .
   a at home   b on vacation   c at work
2 _____ are talking on the telephone.
   a Kate's parents   b Kate's friends   c Kate's brothers
3 They are in _____ .
   a Boston   b Los Angeles   c London
4 Kate has _____ and a sister.
   a no brothers   b one brother   c two brothers

B ▶ 2.17 Watch or listen again, and answer the questions.

1 What time is it in London? _____
2 What time is it in Los Angeles? _____

Conversation builder | telling the time

Asking for the time:
What time is it?   What time's the movie?
What's the time?   What time's the next bus?

Talking about times:
It's ten o'clock.   The movie is at eight thirty.
It's seven a.m./p.m.   The bus is in ten minutes.

3 A Read the Conversation builder. Match the questions with pictures a–d.

1 What's the time? _____
2 What time is CSI Miami? _____
3 What time is it in New York? _____
4 What time's the train to Stamford? _____

B Ask and answer the questions in pairs.

asking for information politely ■ telling the time   **SPEAKING**   SKILLS   **2D**

4 ▶ 2.18 Watch or listen to the rest of the show. Match the times in the box with the people.

8:15   9:00   3:00   8:45   12:30

 Man 1  Woman 1  Woman 2  Man 2  Simon

5 A ▶ 2.18 Match the questions with the people from exercise 4. Watch or listen again, and check.

1 When's the game? _____
2 OK, what time is it? _____
3 Excuse me. What time's the *James Bond* movie? _____
4 Excuse me. What time is it, please? _____
5 Where's the number 67 bus? _____

B Which questions are polite? Why?

> **Skill**   asking for information politely
>
> When you ask for information, it's important to be polite.
> • Use *Excuse me* to get the person's attention.
> • At the end of the conversation, say *Thank you* or *Thanks*.
> • If you want to be extra polite, say *Please* at the end of questions.

6 ▶ 2.19 Read the Skill box. In pairs, guess the missing words from the conversations. Listen and check.

Woman 1 ¹_____ . What time is it, ²_____ ?
Kate It's 8:15. Quarter past.
Woman 1 Oh! I'm late. ³_____ very much.

Woman 2 ⁴_____ , what time is the number 67 bus?
Kate Next bus ... 8:45. It's in ten minutes.
Woman 2 Oh, 8:45, not 8:35. Ten minutes. OK. ⁵_____ .

7 In pairs, practice asking for information politely.

Questions	Answers
what / the teacher's name	It's Leanne.
what time / next bus to Chicago	It's at 12:20 p.m.
where / the museum	It's that building.
what / name of this restaurant	It's The Golden Dragon.
what / the school's phone number	It's 354 269.

Go to Communication practice: Student A page 135, Student B page 143

8 A PREPARE In pairs, choose the movie theater or the airport and invent the missing information.

★ **SILVER MOVIE THEATER** ★

MOVIE TITLE	TIME	SCREEN
Star Wars	_____	_____
Titanic	_____	_____
The Wizard of Oz	_____	_____

Airport departures ✈ 10:05

Flight	Time	Gate
Stockholm	_____	_____
Beijing	_____	_____
Lima	_____	_____

B PRACTICE In pairs, ask and answer questions about the movies or the flights. Remember to be polite.

C PERSONAL BEST Invent information for the other situation and repeat the activity. Is your speaking better this time?

Personal Best   Write a conversation with a tourist in your local train or bus station.

1 and 2 REVIEW AND PRACTICE

Grammar

1 Choose the correct options to complete the sentences.

1 Hi Laura, I _____ Khalid's brother. Nice to meet you.
 a 's
 b 're
 c 'm

2 How old _____ your grandfather?
 a are
 b is
 c am

3 _____ these your glasses?
 a Am
 b Is
 c Are

4 A Is your sister's boyfriend from Brazil?
 B No, _____ .
 a he's not
 b she's not
 c I'm not

5 A What's this?
 B It's _____ old book.
 a –
 b a
 c an

6 _____ my mother over there with the blue umbrella.
 a These are
 b This is
 c That's

7 My wife's a chef, and this is _____ new restaurant.
 a she's
 b her
 c his

8 My _____ last name is Chen.
 a grandfather's
 b grandfather
 c grandfathers

2 Rewrite the sentences with the new words.

1 He's an English teacher.
 They *'re English teachers* .

2 These are my red pens.
 This _____ .

3 We're happy with our new tablets.
 I _____ .

4 Those expensive cars are Italian.
 That _____ .

5 I'm a student in India.
 She _____ .

6 My brother's an office worker, and this is his backpack.
 My brothers _____ , and these _____ .

3 Choose the correct options to complete the text.

A HOLLYWOOD FAMILY

¹ *These / This* is Zooey Deschanel. She's ² *a / an* actor and a singer. ³ *She / Her* sister Emily is an actor, too. She's in the TV show *Bones*. What ⁴ *'s / 're* their mother's job? An actor. And ⁵ *their / our* father's job? ⁶ *Her / His* job is in movies too! That's not all – Zooey's ⁷ *sister's / sisters* husband is … an actor. They ⁸ *'re / 's* from California in the U.S., and they're a Hollywood family. They ⁹ *are / 're not* the only family like this. From Marlon Brando's family to Will Smith's family, they ¹⁰ *'m / 're* easy to find in Hollywood.

Vocabulary

1 Put the words in the box in the correct columns.

| difficult engineer grandfather interesting IT worker cell phone mother pencil receptionist small watch wife |

Jobs	Adjectives	Family	Personal items
	difficult		

REVIEW and PRACTICE 1 and 2

2 Circle the word that is different. Explain your answers.
1 black   new   orange   gold
2 chef   tour guide TV host   grandmother
3 French   Polish   Russian   Canada
4 fifty   thirteen   fourteen   seventeen
5 son   glasses   change   keys
6 Hi   Bye   Hello   Good morning
7 bad   boring   ugly   happy
8 father   daughter   boyfriend   husband

3 Choose the correct options to complete the sentences.
1 Jing Wei is _____ . She's from Shanghai.
   a doctor   b Chinese   c brother
2 Excuse me, what does "building" _____ ?
   a say   b understand   c mean
3 My sister's daughter is six, and her _____ is four.
   a son   b children   c husband
4 That camera is very _____ .
   a new   b young   c sad
5 Russia is a very _____ country.
   a small   b easy   c big
6 I'm from _____ . I'm American.
   a the UK   b the U.S.   c Argentina
7 A It's nine fifteen.
   B Sorry I'm _____ .
   a student   b teacher   c late
8 Macu is a _____ . She's in her car all day.
   a salesclerk   b taxi driver   c girlfriend
9 A What color is a chef's hat?
   B It's _____ .
   a white   b small   c pink
10 The pages of this old _____ are yellow.
   a tablet   b wallet   c book

4 Complete the conversation with the words in the box.

| nineteen | Germany | Italian | waitress |
| backpack | student | girlfriend | later |

Max Who's that girl with Frank? Is she his sister?
Sue No. That's his new ¹_____ .
Max Wow! Is she from here?
Sue No, she's from ²_____ .
Max She's beautiful. How old is she?
Sue She's ³_____ .
Max Is she a college ⁴_____ ?
Sue No, she's a ⁵_____ at the ⁶_____ restaurant on Green Street.
Max Oh no, I'm late for class. See you ⁷_____ .
Sue Hey ... is that your ⁸_____ ?
Max Yes, it is. Thanks!
Sue Bye.

23

UNIT 3
Food and drink

LANGUAGE simple present (*I, you, we, they*) ■ food and drink

3A Food for athletes

1 ▶ 3.1 Put the words in the box in the correct columns. Listen and check.

| eggs   orange juice   meat   tea   coffee   bread   rice   water |

We eat ...	We drink ...

Go to Vocabulary practice: food and drink, page 112

2 In pairs, talk about food and drink that you like and don't like.

　😊 *I like meat.*　　　☹ *I don't like coffee.*

3 **A** Look at the pictures. What food can you see? Is it healthy?

　B Match pictures a and b with the athletes. Read the text quickly and check.

Olympic Diets
What do Olympic athletes eat for breakfast, lunch, and dinner? We talk to two very different athletes.

Artem Petrenko, Weightlifter, Ukraine

What do you have for breakfast?
For breakfast, I eat six eggs and three or four cheese sandwiches. I drink a liter of orange juice and three cups of coffee.

What about lunch and dinner?
I have lunch at 1:00 p.m. I eat a big bowl of pasta or rice, and salad. For dinner, I eat meat – with potatoes and vegetables. During the day, I eat more sandwiches and fruit.

That's a lot of food! What's your favorite food?
Cheese. I love all cheese, and my favorite is Dutch cheese, like Gouda.

Michelle Nelson, Marathon runner, Australia

What do you have for breakfast?
For breakfast, I eat whole wheat bread and fruit, and I drink "green juice" – it's juice with green vegetables and fruit. I'm a vegan, so I don't eat meat, eggs, or fish, and I don't drink milk.

What about lunch and dinner?
For lunch, I have a vegan burger with rice and salad. In the evening, I have dinner with my family. It's difficult because we don't like the same things! But we all eat pizza. My two sisters like cheese, but I have a vegan pizza – without cheese!

Do marathon runners eat dessert?
Yes, they do! Well, maybe not all of them ... but I love dessert. It's my favorite part of the meal. I love carrot cake and vegan ice cream.

simple present (*I, you, we, they*) ■ food and drink **LANGUAGE 3A**

4 Read the text again and complete the sentences with the correct words.
1 What _____ you _____ for breakfast?
2 I _____ a liter of orange juice.
3 I _____ lunch at 1:00 p.m.
4 I _____ milk.
5 We _____ the same things.
6 _____ marathon runners _____ dessert?

5 A Look at the sentences in exercise 4 and answer the questions.
1 Which sentences are affirmative? ____ and ____
2 Which are negative? ____ and ____
3 Which are questions? ____ and ____

B Complete the rules. Then read the Grammar box.
1 We use _____ + verb in negative simple present sentences with *I, you, we,* and *they*.
2 We use _____ + subject + verb in simple present questions with *I, you, we,* and *they*.

Grammar simple present (*I, you, we, they*)

Affirmative:
I **drink** a lot of water.
We **eat** ice cream for dessert.

Negative:
You **don't drink** coffee.
They **don't like** vegetables.

Questions and short answers:
Do you **like** fish?
Yes, I **do**. No, I **don't**.

Go to Grammar practice: simple present (*I, you, we, they*), page 98

6 ▶ 3.4 **Pronunciation:** *do you* /dəyuw/ Listen and repeat the questions. Pay attention to the pronunciation of *do you* /dəyuw/.
1 Do you like pizza?   2 What do you eat for breakfast?   3 What food do you like?

7 A ▶ 3.5 Say the questions. Listen, check, and repeat.
1 Do you like Mexican food?
2 Do you eat meat?
3 Do you drink tea?
4 Do you like chocolate?
5 What time do you have breakfast?
6 What do you have for lunch?

B Ask and answer the questions in pairs.

8 A ▶ 3.6 Complete the text with the verbs in parentheses. Listen and check.

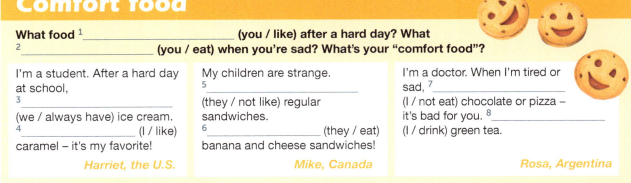

Comfort food

What food ¹_____ (you / like) after a hard day? What
²_____ (you / eat) when you're sad? What's your "comfort food"?

I'm a student. After a hard day at school, ³_____ (we / always have) ice cream. ⁴_____ (I / like) caramel – it's my favorite!
Harriet, the U.S.

My children are strange. ⁵_____ (they / not like) regular sandwiches. ⁶_____ (they / eat) banana and cheese sandwiches!
Mike, Canada

I'm a doctor. When I'm tired or sad, ⁷_____ (I / not eat) chocolate or pizza – it's bad for you. ⁸_____ (I / drink) green tea.
Rosa, Argentina

B In pairs, talk about your "comfort food." What do you eat or drink when you're sad or tired?

Go to Communication practice: Student A page 136, Student B page 144

9 A Ask and answer questions in pairs.
1 like / Japanese food
2 drink / a lot of soda
3 have / dinner with your family
4 eat / a lot of fruit
5 drink / coffee at night
6 eat / a lot of red meat

A *Do you like Japanese food?*   **B** *No, I don't. But I like Chinese food.*

B Tell the class what you and your partner have in common.
We don't like Japanese food, but we like Chinese food.

Personal Best Write what you have for breakfast, lunch, and dinner on a typical day.

25

3 SKILLS   LISTENING   listening for times and days ■ /ə/ ■ days and times of day

3B Tea or coffee?

1 Complete the café sign with the days of the week.

Friday   Tuesday   Wednesday   Sunday

Go to Vocabulary practice: days and times of day, page 116

2 Look at the sign in exercise 1 again. Are the sentences true (T) or false (F)?

1 The café is open every day. ____
2 It's open in the morning on Tuesdays. ____
3 It's open on Thursday afternoons. ____
4 It's open in the evening on Fridays. ____
5 It's closed on Saturday nights. ____
6 It's closed in the evening on Sundays. ____

3 Ask and answer the questions in pairs.

1 What day is it today?
2 What day is it tomorrow?
3 What day was it yesterday?
4 What's your favorite day of the week?
5 What's the worst day of the week?
6 What's your favorite time of day?

4 A ▶ 3.8   Watch or listen to the first part of the show. Check (✓) the sentence which is correct.

1 People drink coffee in cafés and tea at home. ☐
2 People drink tea and coffee all over the world. ☐
3 People drink coffee in the morning and tea in the evening. ☐

B ▶ 3.8   Watch or listen again. Match the parts to make sentences.

1 54% of Americans
2 65% of those people
3 35% of those people
4 In the UK, people drink 165 million
5 In the UK, people drink 70 million

a cups of tea every day.
b drink coffee at lunch or later.
c drink coffee every day.
d drink coffee in the morning.
e cups of coffee every day.

listening for times and days ■ /ə/ ■ days and times of day **LISTENING**   **SKILLS 3B**

5 ▶ 3.9 Watch or listen to the second part of the show. Match the people with the food and drink.

 Jolene
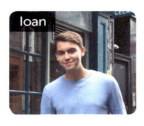 Ioan
 Chan
 Ethan
 Kate

1 fish, rice, vegetables, tea, water _____
2 cookies, ice cream, coffee _____
3 fish and chips and tea _____
4 sandwich, chips, cookie, tea _____
5 coffee, cereal _____

Skill   listening for times and days

Listen carefully when people talk about times and days.
- Times and days can come at the beginning or end of a sentence: *On Friday, I go to the café. / I go to the café on Friday.*
- Some times and days sound similar: *It's three fifteen. / It's three fifty.   Today is Tuesday. / Today is Thursday.*

6 ▶ 3.9 Read the Skill box. Watch or listen again, and choose the correct options to complete the sentences.

1 **Kate:** It's *2:30 p.m. / 2:40 p.m.* here, and I'm with Jolene.
2 **Jolene:** We come here every *Tuesday / Thursday*. It's my husband's favorite café.
3 **Jolene:** I drink coffee every *morning / evening*, but between 2:30 and *3:00 / 3:30*, I drink tea.
4 **Ioan:** The party's at *8:00 p.m. / 9:00 p.m.*
5 **Chan:** We're open *Monday / Sunday* through Friday from 11:00 a.m. until 10:00 p.m. And Saturday and Sunday from 10:00 a.m. until *7:00 p.m. / 11:00 p.m.*
6 **Kate:** It's *3:15 / 3:30* here, and I have fish and chips from my favorite takeaway place!

7 In pairs, talk about what food and drink you have every day.
I have a coffee at 10:00 in the morning.

8 ▶ 3.10 Listen to the extract from the show. How does Ethan pronounce *and*?

*I have a coffee **and** cereal.*

Listening builder /ə/

The /ə/ sound is also called "schwa." It is very common in English in short unstressed words, like articles, prepositions, and auxiliary verbs.

/ə/ /ə/   /ə/   /ə/   /ə/
a cup *of* tea We have coffee *at* 9:00 p.m. What time's *the* party? *Does* she like fish?

9 ▶ 3.11 Read the Listening builder. Then listen and complete the sentences.
1 I have _____ coffee every morning.
2 What _____ they eat?
3 They only drink coffee _____ breakfast.
4 This one's _____ you.
5 I have two bottles _____ water.
6 I like burgers _____ French fries.

10 Think of a café that you like. In pairs, ask and answer the questions about the café.

What's its name?   Where is it?   When do you go there?
What do you eat or drink there?   What do other people have?   Why do you like it?

Personal Best Write a description of your favorite restaurant or café.

27

3 LANGUAGE — simple present (*he, she, it*) ■ common verbs (1)

3C Chocolate for breakfast!

1 Complete phrases 1–6 with the verbs in the box.

use   watch   have   go   make   say

1 ____ "hello"   2 ____ a cat   3 ____ dinner   4 ____ running   5 ____ a computer   6 ____ TV

Personal Best

Go to Vocabulary practice: common verbs (1), page 113

2 Ask and answer the questions in pairs.

1 you / live near downtown?
2 you / work in an office?
3 you / make dinner at home every evening?
4 you / know three languages?
5 you / say "hello" to a lot of people every day?
6 you / have brothers or sisters?

3 ▶ 3.13   Look at the picture of Adam Young. What is his job? Read and listen to the text and check.

THE BEST JOB IN THE WORLD?

From Monday through Friday, Adam Young eats chocolate at work. That's because Adam is a *chocolatier* (he makes chocolate). "I love it," he says. "I think it's a great job!" Adam lives in Brooklyn in New York. He has a small store, and he makes all of his chocolates by hand. Does he have the best job in the world? This is his typical day. "In the morning, I go to the store early and make chocolate … I eat it for breakfast! Then we work here all day."

Adam has an assistant, Jenny. When he's in the kitchen with the chocolate, Jenny works with the customers.
Adam exercises a lot – very important when you eat chocolate all day! In the evening, he changes his clothes and goes to the gym. Then he goes home, makes dinner, and watches TV.
On the weekend, he studies business – he says it's important for his job … but he doesn't eat chocolate!

4 A Choose the correct words to complete the sentences. What letter do we add to the verbs with *he*, *she*, and *it* in affirmative sentences?

1 Adam Young *eat / eats* chocolate at work.
2 He *make / makes* all of his chocolates by hand.
3 I go to the store early and *make / makes* chocolate.
4 I *eat / eats* it for breakfast!
5 Then we *work / works* here all day.
6 Jenny *work / works* with the customers.

B Find the *he/she/it* forms of the verbs in the text.

1 say _____   3 have _____   5 change _____   7 watch _____
2 live _____   4 exercise _____   6 go _____   8 study _____

28

simple present (*he, she, it*) ■ common verbs (1)   LANGUAGE **3C**

5 Find a question and a negative sentence in the text. Complete the rules, and then read the Grammar box.

1 We use _____ + verb in negative simple present sentences with *he/she/it*.
2 We use _____ + subject + verb in simple present questions with *he/she/it*.

📖 **Grammar** simple present (*he, she, it*)

Affirmative:	Negative:	Questions and short answers:
She **eats** fruit for breakfast.	He **doesn't work** in a school.	**Does** your house **have** a yard?
He **watches** TV in the evening.	She **doesn't exercise**.	Yes, it **does**. No, it **doesn't**.
Maya **studies** English.	My wife **doesn't like** chocolate.	

Look! Some verbs are irregular: *do > does, go > goes, have > has*.

Go to Grammar practice: simple present (*he, she, it*), page 98

6 A ▶ 3.15 **Pronunciation:** *-s* and *-es* endings   Listen and repeat the sounds and words. Pay attention to the pronunciation of the *-s* and *-es* endings.

1 /s/   eats   works   makes
2 /z/   lives   goes   knows
3 /ɪz/   watches   uses   changes

B ▶ 3.16 Match the parts to make sentences. Listen, check, and repeat.

1 She lives   a movies in the afternoon.
2 He works   b in an office.
3 She watches   c a computer at work.
4 He says   d "Hi" every day.
5 She makes   e in Tokyo.
6 He uses   f cakes on the weekend.

7 ▶ 3.17 Complete the text with the correct form of the verbs in the box. Listen and check.

have   exercise   eat   say   work   make   go

A VERY COOL JOB
Kirsten Lind ¹_____ for an ice cream company in Toronto. She ²_____ a great job – she's a food scientist, and she ³_____ new flavors of ice cream. What's this week's new flavor? "Potato chips and chocolate! I don't like potato chips, but lots of people love it," Kirsten ⁴_____ . Kirsten ⁵_____ two or three liters of ice cream a week, so she ⁶_____ to the gym after work, and she ⁷_____ a lot on the weekend.

8 A Make questions about the text in exercise 7.

1 Kirsten / work / in a store?   _____
2 she / have / an interesting job?   _____
3 she / eat / a lot of potato chips?   _____
4 she / exercise / a lot?   _____

B Ask and answer the questions in pairs. Use short answers.

Go to Communication practice: Student A page 136, Student B page 144

9 Choose three friends or family members and write down their names. Ask and answer the questions in pairs.

A *Who is Ivan?*   B *He's my uncle.*
A *Where does he live?*   B *He lives in ...*

Who is … ?   Where does he/she live?   Where does he/she work?
Does he/she like his/her job?   What does he/she do on the weekend?

Personal Best   Think of someone with an interesting job and write a paragraph about him/her.

29

3 SKILLS WRITING punctuation ■ linking words (*and*, *but*)

3D A special meal

1 A Match the food in the box with the celebrations in the pictures. What do you know about these celebration

pancakes   chow mein   turkey   candy

Thanksgiving, U.S.   Carnevale, Italy   Chinese New Year, China   Maslenitsa, Russia

B Think of some important celebrations and festivals in your country. What do people eat and drink?

2 Look at the pictures in Arusha's blog. What country is she from? How do people celebrate this festival? Read the text quickly and check.

Arusha's Blog

MY POSTS | CONTACT ME | SEARCH

About me
Hi! I'm Arusha, I'm 25, and I live in Kerala in India. Welcome to my blog!

Festival time
We have lots of festivals in India, and my favorite is Onam.
In the afternoon, we have a big meal with lots of food – some people have 24 dishes or more. We eat curry, rice, vegetables, and fruit, but we don't eat meat. We eat the food on a big banana leaf.

It's traditional to have lunch at home, but these days some people go to restaurants. In my family, we eat at my brother's house. After the meal, we meet friends, we listen to music, and we watch the tiger dance. What's my favorite thing about Onam? It's a really happy time, and the food is great.

3 Read the text again and answer the questions.
1 What is the name of the festival?
2 When do people have the meal?
3 What food does Arusha eat?
4 What doesn't she eat?
5 Where does she have lunch?
6 What does she do after the meal?

punctuation ■ linking words (*and*, *but*) **WRITING** SKILLS **3D**

4 Read the Skill box. Find an example of each type of punctuation in the text on page 30.

🔧 Skill · punctuation

It's important to use the correct punctuation to help people understand your writing.

.	**period:**	We use this at the end of a sentence.
,	**comma:**	We use this to separate ideas and after times.
?	**question mark:**	We use this at the end of a question.
'	**apostrophe:**	We use this in contractions and in 's for possession.
A	**capital letters:**	(see the Text builder on page 13)

5 Rewrite the text about Chinese New Year with the correct punctuation and capital letters.

whats your favorite festival

my names wu and im from nanjing in china my favorite festival is chinese new year its a national holiday and people dont work we have a big party with all the family and in the evening we eat meat fish rice and vegetables my mother makes a special cake and we give money to the children in the family

6 Choose the correct words to complete the sentences from Arusha's blog. Check your answers in the text.
   1 We eat curry, rice, vegetables, and fruit, *and / but* we don't eat meat.
   2 It's a really happy time, *and / but* the food is great.

🧩 Text builder · linking words (*and*, *but*)

We use *and* and *but* to link sentences.
To add information: *We dance **and** we listen to music.*
To contrast different ideas: *Some people go to restaurants, **but** our family eats at home.*

7 Read the Text builder. Complete the sentences with *and* or *but*.
   1 We go to my grandmother's house every Sunday, _____ we have a big meal.
   2 This restaurant is expensive, _____ the food isn't very good.
   3 I drink tea and fruit juice, _____ I don't drink coffee.
   4 Claire works in the morning, _____ she doesn't work in the afternoon.
   5 My uncle lives in Los Angeles, _____ he's not American.
   6 He exercises, _____ he goes to the gym.

8 A **PREPARE** Choose a festival or celebration in your country where food is important. Think about these questions.
   • When is the festival or celebration?
   • What do people eat and drink?
   • Where do you eat and who do you eat with?
   • What do you do before and after the meal?

   B **PRACTICE** Write a blog about the festival or celebration. Link your sentences with *and* and *but*.

   C **PERSONAL BEST** Exchange your blog with your partner. Check the grammar and punctuation. Are the simple present verbs correct? Does your partner use *and* and *but* correctly?

Personal Best Think of a special meal. Write three sentences about it with *and*, and three sentences with *but*.

UNIT 4 Daily life

LANGUAGE frequency adverbs ■ daily routine verbs

4A Day and night

1 A 🔊 4.1 Match the phrases in the box with pictures a–e. Listen and check.

| start work   finish work   go to bed   get home   get up |

B In pairs, say what time you do the activities.

A *I get up at 6:30.*   **B** *That's early! I get up at 8:30.*

Go to Vocabulary practice: daily routine verbs, page 114

2 Look at the pictures and guess the answers to the questions. Read the text and check.
1 What is the relationship between the two people?
2 What are their jobs?
3 Are their routines similar or different?

The same but different

Sally and Ashley Fraser live at home with their parents and their brother, Marcus. They are twin sisters … but their lives are very different.

"I'm a receptionist for a big company, and I always get up at 6:00 a.m.," says Sally. "I take a shower, and then I go to work. In the evening, I watch TV, and I usually go to bed early. I never see Ashley – she's at work."

"Sally has a regular job," says Ashley. "I'm a singer, and I often get home really late – at 2:00 or 3:00 a.m. I get up at 11:00 or 12:00, and I sometimes see friends in the afternoon."

The twins are different, but are they friends?
"Yes, we are!" says Sally. "We're always together on Sunday!"

3 Complete the sentences with the frequency adverbs in the box. Check your answers in the text.

| always   sometimes   usually   never   often |

1 I _____ see Ashley.
2 I _____ see friends in the afternoon.
3 I _____ get home really late.
4 I _____ go to bed early.
5 I _____ get up at 6:00 a.m.

frequency adverbs ■ daily routine verbs   LANGUAGE   4A

4 A Put the frequency adverbs in the box in the correct order.

sometimes   usually   never

100% ———————————————————————————————— 0%
always   1_____   often   2_____   3_____

B Read the sentences in exercise 3 again. Do the frequency adverbs come before or after the verbs? Read the Grammar box.

Grammar frequency adverbs

100%
always: I **always** have breakfast at home.
usually: She **usually** takes a shower in the morning.
often: I **often** get up late on the weekend.
sometimes: I **sometimes** get home at 1:00 a.m.
0%
never: She **never** has dinner at home.

Look! Frequency adverbs come after the verb *be*: We're **always** together on Sunday.

Go to Grammar practice: frequency adverbs, page 99

5 A 4.4 **Pronunciation:** sentence stress Listen to the sentences. Are the frequency adverbs stressed or unstressed?

1 I usually get up at 7:00 a.m.
2 I always have a cup of coffee for breakfast.
3 I never go to the gym.
4 I often make dinner in the evening.

B Listen again, check, and repeat.

6 Change the frequency adverbs in 5A so the sentences are true for you.
In pairs, say the sentences with the correct stress.
A *I sometimes get up at 7:00 a.m.*   **B** *Really? I never get up at 7:00 a.m.*

7 A Look at the chart. Write five sentences about Sally and Ashley's brother, Marcus.
He always has breakfast in a café.

	Mon	Tue	Wed	Thu	Fri
1 have breakfast in a café	✓	✓	✓	✓	✓
2 watch TV in the morning	✓	✗	✓	✗	✓
3 work in the evening	✓	✗	✓	✓	✓
4 see friends after work	✗	✗	✗	✗	✓
5 go to bed before midnight	✗	✗	✗	✗	✗

B 4.5 Listen and check. What is Marcus's job?

Go to Communication practice: Student A page 136, Student B page 144

8 In pairs, compare yourself with members of your family. Use the activities in the boxes.
I always get up before 7:00 a.m., but my brother usually gets up late, at 9:30.

get up before 7:00 a.m.   eat fast food   watch TV in the morning   go to bed late

get home before 6:00 p.m.   have coffee for breakfast   have lunch at work   take a shower in the morning

Personal Best Describe your typical routine on the weekend.

33

4 SKILLS

READING finding specific information ■ 's: possession or contraction ■ transportation

4B My trip to work

1 Match the types of transportation with pictures a–e on page 35.

1 bike _____   4 car _____
2 taxi _____   5 subway _____
3 bus _____

Go to Vocabulary practice: transportation, page 115

2 Look at the pictures and the title of the text on page 35. Guess the answers to the questions. Read the text quickly and check.

1 What city is it about?   2 What type of transportation is it about?

🔧 Skill · finding specific information

We sometimes need to find specific information in a text.
- Read the questions carefully to see what information you need to find.
- Find the place in the text which has this information and read it carefully.
- Don't worry if you don't understand every word.

3 A Read the Skill box. Then find information in the paragraph about Emily in the text to complete the first line of the chart.

	Lives where?	Which job?	Works where?
Emily	*Harlem*		
Dan			
Megan			
Walter			

B Now find the information about the other people in the text. Complete the chart.

4 Read the text again. Then, in pairs, say why each person uses a *citibike*.

Emily uses a citibike because it's fast.

5 Complete the sentences from the text. In which sentences does 's mean *is*?

1 _____ office is in Downtown Manhattan.
2 "The _____ cheap," she says.

✦ Text builder · 's: possession or contraction

If you see *'s* at the end of a word, decide if it refers to possession or if it is a contraction of *is*.
*The **city's** blue public bikes* = possession (the bikes belong to the city)
***Megan's** a waitress on the Lower East Side* = contraction (Megan is a waitress)

6 Read the Text builder. Then read the sentences and write *P* (possession) or *C* (contraction).

1 Ravi's a doctor. _____
2 David's mom is a teacher. _____
3 My train's always late. _____
4 Julia's brother starts work at 7:00. _____

7 Discuss the questions in pairs.

1 Do you have public bikes in your town or city? Are they popular? Why/Why not?
2 How do you usually travel to work or school?
3 Do you like the trip? Why/Why not?

Personal Best

34

finding specific information ■ 's: possession or contraction ■ transportation   READING   SKILLS   4B

A morning in the life of bike 0827

New York is famous for its yellow taxis and noisy subway, but a lot of people also travel by *citibike* – the city's blue public bikes. New Yorkers make 14 million trips a year on *citibikes*. Who uses them and why? We follow one bike for a morning to find out.

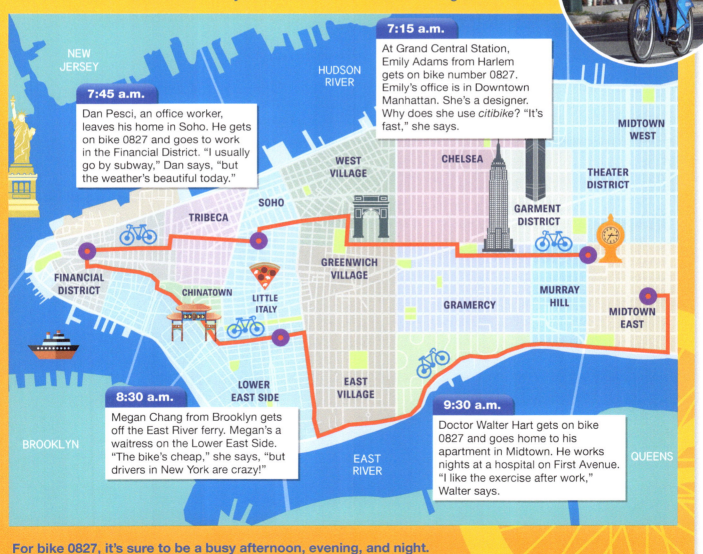

7:15 a.m.
At Grand Central Station, Emily Adams from Harlem gets on bike number 0827. Emily's office is in Downtown Manhattan. She's a designer. Why does she use *citibike*? "It's fast," she says.

7:45 a.m.
Dan Pesci, an office worker, leaves his home in Soho. He gets on bike 0827 and goes to work in the Financial District. "I usually go by subway," Dan says, "but the weather's beautiful today."

8:30 a.m.
Megan Chang from Brooklyn gets off the East River ferry. Megan's a waitress on the Lower East Side. "The bike's cheap," she says, "but drivers in New York are crazy!"

9:30 a.m.
Doctor Walter Hart gets on bike 0827 and goes home to his apartment in Midtown. He works nights at a hospital on First Avenue. "I like the exercise after work," Walter says.

For bike 0827, it's sure to be a busy afternoon, evening, and night.

Personal Best Write about the different types of transportation in your town or city.

4 LANGUAGE simple present: *wh-* questions ■ adjectives (2)

4C Where do you work?

1 Match the adjectives in the box with their opposites.

> quiet   clean   hot   fast   unfriendly

1 dirty / _____   2 cold / _____   3 friendly / _____   4 noisy / _____   5 slow / _____

Go to Vocabulary practice: adjectives (2), page 116

2 A Write down two examples for each of these things.

> a cold country   a large building in your country   a noisy job   a long river   a fast animal
> a friendly café or store in your town or city   a hot drink   a quiet place in your town or city

B Compare your answers in pairs. Do you have the same things?

3 Read the text quickly and answer the questions.

1 What is Tess's job? _____
2 Does she like her job? _____
3 What time does she start work? _____
4 Where does she live? _____

A Dirty Job?

 Tess Mitchell is a garbage collector. It's dirty work, and she gets up very early, but she loves her job.

What time do you start work?
I start work at 5:00 in the morning. I get up at 4:15 a.m. and have breakfast. Then I leave for work.

¹_____ do you work?
I work in south Chicago. The landfill isn't far from my house.

²_____ do you do on a typical day?
I drive the truck to about 800 houses every day from Monday through Friday. That's a lot of trash!

³_____ do you like the job?
Because the people are friendly and I work outside. Sometimes it's very cold early in the morning, but when the weather's nice, I love it.

⁴_____ do you finish work?
I finish at 1:30 p.m. I'm a mom, so the hours are great. I get home at 2:00, take a shower, and then I go to my children's school to pick them up.

⁵_____ do you relax when you're not at work?
I play soccer with a women's soccer team, and we practice on Tuesday and Thursday evenings. On the weekend, I get up late!

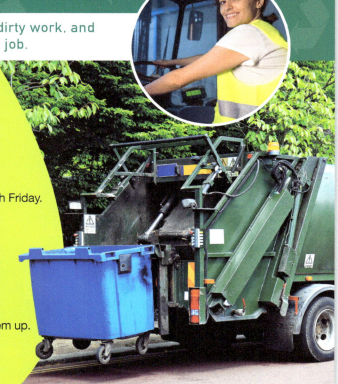

simple present: *wh-* questions ■ adjectives (2)   **LANGUAGE 4C**

4 A Complete the questions in the text with the question words in the box. How do you say them in your language?

Why   Where   When   What   How

B Look at the questions in the text again. Order the words below from 1–4 to make a question. Then read the Grammar box.

☐ *do/does*   ☐ main verb   ☐ question word   ☐ subject

📖 **Grammar** simple present: *wh-* questions

Question word:	*do/does*:	Subject:	Main verb:
Where	do	you	live?
What	does	your husband	do?
How	does	he	get to work?
When	do	your children	watch TV?
What time	do	they	get up?
Why	do	you	work on the weekend?
Who	do	you	work with?

Go to Grammar practice: simple present: *wh-* questions, page 99

5 ▶ 4.10 **Pronunciation:** question words Listen and repeat the question words. Do they begin with a /w/ sound or a /h/ sound?

1 where ____   2 when ____   3 who ____   4 why ____   5 how ____   6 what ____

6 A ▶ 4.11 Order the words to make questions. Say the questions with the correct pronunciation of the question words. Listen, check, and repeat.

1 you / have / how many / do / children _____?
2 what / they / time / have breakfast / do _____?
3 do / does / husband / your / what _____?
4 he / when / does / work _____?
5 on the weekend / you / what / do / do _____?

B ▶ 4.12 Match questions 1–5 with answers a–e. Listen to the interview with Tess and check.

a In the afternoons and evenings.
b Two.
c He's a taxi driver.
d 7:30.
e We often go to the park.

Go to Communication practice: Student A page 137, Student B page 145

7 A Find out about your partner. Ask and answer the questions in the boxes in pairs.

| What time / start work? | Who / live with? | How / get to your English classes? |

| What / have for breakfast? | Where / usually go on vacation? | How / relax in the evening? |

| Why / study English? | When / do your English homework? | How many brothers and sisters / have? |

B Switch partners. Ask and answer questions about your first partner.

A *What time does Sasha start work?*   **B** *He usually starts work at 8:00 a.m.*

Personal Best Write ten questions for an interview with an actor/singer that you like.   37

4 SKILLS SPEAKING being polite in stores ■ grocery shopping

4D How can I help you?

1 A ▶ 4.13 Match the prices with the words. Listen and check.

a £5   b $50   c €15   d £5.95   e 50p   f 50c
g $19.99   h $9.99   i $25   j $11.99   k $6.50   l $29

1 nine dollars ninety-nine _____
2 nineteen dollars ninety-nine _____
3 fifteen euros _____
4 fifty dollars _____
5 eleven dollars ninety-nine _____
6 twenty-nine dollars _____
7 fifty pence _____
8 five pounds _____
9 six dollars fifty _____
10 fifty cents _____
11 five pounds ninety-five _____
12 twenty-five dollars _____

B Write down three prices in numbers and give them to your partner. Say your partner's prices.

That's three dollars fifty.

2 Discuss the questions in pairs.
1 Who usually goes grocery shopping in your house?
2 Where do you usually buy groceries? Why?
   a at a supermarket   b at a market   c at local stores
3 Do you like grocery shopping? Why/Why not?

3 ▶ 4.14 Watch or listen to the first part of *Learning Curve*. Are the sentences true (T) or false (F)?

1 Penny likes grocery shopping. _____
2 Penny and Taylor live together. _____
3 They usually go grocery shopping on Thursdays. _____
4 There is a big supermarket near their apartment. _____

Penny

4 ▶ 4.15 Watch or listen to the second part of the show. Check (✓) the things Penny buys and the correct prices.

store 1	store 2	store 3
half a chicken ☐	cheese and salad ☐	a blue shopping cart ☐
a whole chicken ☐	cheese and eggs ☐	a black shopping cart ☐
$4.79 ☐	$17.15 ☐	$21.77 ☐
$8.79 ☐	$17.50 ☐	$22.02 ☐

5 ▶ 4.15 Who says the phrases: Penny (P), Salesclerk 1 (S1), Salesclerk 2 (S2), or Salesclerk 3 (S3)? Watch or listen again, and check.

1 How much is it for that small shopping cart? _____
2 Here you go. _____
3 I'd like a whole chicken, please. _____
4 You're welcome. _____
5 Here's your change – 25 cents. _____
6 Can I have two pounds of this white cheese? _____

being polite in stores ■ grocery shopping **SPEAKING** SKILLS **4D**

Conversation builder — grocery shopping

Customer:
Do you have …?
Can I have …
I'd like …
How much is that?
Here you go/are.

Salesclerk:
How can I help you?
Anything else?
That's … dollars.
Here you are.
Here's your change.
Have a nice day!

6 A Read the Conversation builder. Then, order the sentences from 1–7 to make a conversation in a store.

- a ☐ Yes. Anything else?
- b ☐ Yes, I'd like five cookies, please. How much is that?
- c ☐ Can I have a chocolate cake, please?
- d ☐ Thanks. And here's your change.
- e ☐ Here you are – $10.
- f ☐ Hello. How can I help you?
- g ☐ That's $8.50.

B ▶ 4.16 Listen and check. Practice the conversation in pairs.

7 ▶ 4.17 Complete the conversation with the words in the box. Listen and check. Are Penny and the salesclerk polite? Why/Why not?

welcome   good   thank you   please

Salesclerk	¹_____ evening.	**Penny**	³_____ .
Penny	I'd like a whole chicken, ²_____ .	**Salesclerk**	You're ⁴_____ .
Salesclerk	Here you are.		

Skill — being polite in stores

It's important to be polite if you work in a store or if you're a customer.
- Greet people. Say: *Hi / Good morning / Good evening*, etc.
- Ask for things politely. Say: *Can I have …? / I'd like …, please.* NOT *I want … / Give me …*
- If someone says: *Thanks / Thank you*, you can reply: *You're welcome.*
- Salesclerks often end by saying: *Have a nice day!*

8 ▶ 4.18 Read the Skill box. Listen to three conversations. Check (✓) the people who are polite.

1 a the customer ☐ b the waiter ☐ c both people ☐
2 a the customer ☐ b the salesclerk ☐ c both people ☐
3 a the customer ☐ b the receptionist ☐ c both people ☐

Go to Communication practice: Student A page 137, Student B page 145

9 A PREPARE In pairs, look at the pictures and choose one of the situations. Write down things you can buy there and their prices.

In a restaurant

At a market

In a café

B PRACTICE Decide who is the customer and who is the salesclerk. Act out your conversation.

C PERSONAL BEST Listen to another pair's conversation. Are they polite? What could they do better?

Personal Best Think of your favorite grocery store or café and write a conversation in English there.

3 and 4 REVIEW and PRACTICE

Grammar

1 Check (✓) the correct sentences.

1 a I never finish work at 5:00 p.m.
   b I don't never finish work at 5:00 p.m.
   c I don't finish work never at 5:00 p.m.
2 a He don't go to bed early.
   b He not go to bed early.
   c He doesn't go to bed early.
3 a Do you go to work by car?
   b Does you go to work by car?
   c When you do go to work by car?
4 a We often has eggs for breakfast.
   b We often have eggs for breakfast.
   c We have often eggs for breakfast.
5 a Why do you live with?
   b Who do you live with?
   c How do you live with?
6 a When they do get up?
   b When they get up?
   c When do they get up?
7 a She work in a restaurant in the evening.
   b She do work in a restaurant in the evening.
   c She works in a restaurant in the evening.
8 a Goes he to the gym after work?
   b Does he to the gym after work?
   c Does he go to the gym after work?

2 Order the words to make questions and sentences.

1 your / do / go / children / where / school / to
   _____?
2 have / she / at / does / lunch / home
   _____?
3 always / dinner / we / eat / vegetables / for
   _____.
4 get / time / what / weekend / do / up / the / you / on
   _____?
5 don't / shopping / I / Saturdays / go / on
   _____.
6 the / he / book / sometimes / a / reads / train / on
   _____.
7 Mondays / quiet / restaurant / is / on / often / the
   _____.
8 in / radio / do / listen / to / you / the / morning / the
   _____?
9 old / brother's / is / how / your / girlfriend
   _____?
10 the / never / exercises / Simon / weekend / on
   _____.

3 Complete the text with the correct form of the verbs in parentheses.

Life on Muck

 This is Laura Marriner. She lives and works on the very small island of Muck in Scotland. Life isn't easy, but it's very interesting …

What ¹_____ (be) Laura's job?
She's a teacher. Her school only ²_____ (have) eight children.

Where ³_____ she _____ (live)?
Laura ⁴_____ (not leave) home in the morning because she lives in the school with her husband and two sons!

How ⁵_____ they _____ (go) shopping?
By ferry. The trip is two hours, but people on the island only ⁶_____ (use) the ferry when the weather is good. They ⁷_____ (not go) shopping every day, so Laura ⁸_____ (make) bread at home.

What is school life like on Muck?
It's great. The children often ⁹_____ (study) on the beach.

¹⁰_____ Laura _____ (like) life on Muck?
Yes, she does! When the weather is bad, life is difficult, but she's happy there. The people are very friendly, and life is an adventure.

Vocabulary

1 Put the words in the box in the correct columns.

| ~~boat~~ ~~cold~~ ~~do~~ cheese fast finish get up know small meat noisy short taxi train want |

Verbs	Adjectives	Nouns
do	cold	boat

40

REVIEW and PRACTICE — 3 and 4

2 Circle the word that is different. Explain your answers.

1	car	truck	bus	plane
2	think	use	slow	make
3	Friday	tomorrow	Sunday	Saturday
4	rice	French fries	potato chips	potatoes
5	coffee	milk	fruit	orange juice
6	clean	horrible	unfriendly	dirty
7	cookie	pizza	cake	chocolate
8	work	study	change	dinner

3 Complete the sentences with the correct words.

1 What time do you g*et* home after work?
2 He usually l_____ to the radio at work.
3 I always have b_____ before I leave home in the morning.
4 They w_____ television after dinner.
5 She goes to school by m_____ . It's very fast.
6 In cold weather, I have a h_____ drink in the evening.
7 He never says "hello." He's so u_____ .
8 T_____ in New York are yellow, and in London they're black.
9 I never drink tea or coffee. I only drink w_____ with meals.
10 On W_____ evenings, I go to the gym.

4 Complete the e-mail with the words in the box.

> bike dressed bread friendly get live
> go evening Saturday read

Hi Ana,

How are you? I'm in Cartagena at my grandmother's house this week. It's nice and quiet here. I ¹_____ up late every day, have breakfast, and get ²_____ . Then I go to the shopping mall by ³_____ . I usually buy some ⁴_____ for lunch. The people are very ⁵_____ . In the afternoon, I ⁶_____ to the beach and ⁷_____ a book. In the ⁸_____ , we sometimes have dinner in a restaurant.

I'm here for one week, and then I go home on ⁹_____ ☹ … I want to ¹⁰_____ here!

See you soon.

Bea

Personal Best

Lesson 3A
Name four things people eat or drink for breakfast.

Lesson 4A
Write four sentences about your daily routine with frequency adverbs.

Lesson 3A
Write a sentence about the food you like and don't like.

Lesson 4B
Name six types of transportation.

Lesson 3B
Name the days of the week that begin with "T."

Lesson 4B
Describe a member of your family's bike, car, or motorcycle.

Lesson 3B
Write a sentence about something you do every week.

Lesson 4C
Write three adjectives that describe your town or city.

Lesson 3C
Write an affirmative and a negative sentence about a friend's typical day.

Lesson 4C
Write three questions for your teacher with different question words.

Lesson 3D
Write about the food you eat on a special occasion. Use *and* and *but*.

Lesson 4D
Write a sentence to ask for something to eat and drink in a café.

41

UNIT 5 All about me

LANGUAGE can and can't ■ common verbs (2)

5A When can you start?

1 Complete phrases 1–5 with the verbs in the box.

> swim   speak   drive   play   call

1 _____ a car
2 _____ Chinese
3 _____ the piano
4 _____ a friend
5 _____ in the ocean

Go to Vocabulary practice: common verbs (2), page 117

2 Read the job posting. What do you need for this job?

SYDNEY CITY TOURS: TOUR GUIDE

Help tourists see the beautiful city of Sydney.

Do you know Sydney? Do you like working with people? Can you speak a foreign language? Do you want to work this summer?

If the answer is "Yes," then contact us.

▶ CONTACT

3 ▶ 5.2 Listen to a job interview. Check (✓) the things Georgia can do. Does she get the job?

	Yes	No
1 Can you speak a foreign language?		
2 Can you drive?		
3 Can you work early in the morning?		
4 Can you swim well?		

4 A ▶ 5.2 Match the halves to make sentences. Listen again and check.

1 Some of the people can't
2 I can speak
3 Yes, I
4 No, I
5 When can you

a can.
b start?
c Chinese.
d can't – sorry.
e speak English.

B Choose the correct options to complete the rules. Then read the Grammar box.

1 We use *can* to talk about *abilities / daily routines*.
2 We use *can't* + verb in *questions / negatives*.
3 We use *can* + subject + verb in *questions / negatives*.

can and *can't* ■ common verbs (2) | **LANGUAGE** | **5A**

Grammar *can* and *can't*

Affirmative:
I **can work** this summer.
Georgia **can swim** well.

Negative:
I **can't speak** Chinese.
They **can't cook**.

Questions and short answers:
Can you **speak** a foreign language?
Yes, I **can**.   No, I **can't**.

Go to Grammar practice: *can* and *can't*, page 100

5 ▶5.4 **Pronunciation:** *can* and *can't* Listen and repeat. Pay attention to the difference between *can* /kæn/ or /kən/ and *can't* /kænt/.

1 He can drive.   2 She can't swim.   3 Can you play the guitar?   4 Yes, I can.

6 A ▶5.5 Say the sentences with the correct pronunciation of *can* and *can't*. Listen, check, and repeat.
1 I can swim two kilometers.   3 I can't speak German.   5 I can drive a car.
2 I can't sing well.   4 I can cook Italian food.   6 I can't play the piano.

B Say the sentences in pairs. Say if you think it's true or false for your partner.

A *I can swim two kilometers.*   B *False. You can't swim two kilometers.*
A *You're right. I can't swim.*

7 A Read the job posting. What does an *au pair* do?

B ▶5.6 Emily and Ben are interested in the job. Listen and check (✓) what they can and can't do.

AU PAIR
- **Can you look after children?**
- **Do you like sports and music?**
- **Do you want to work as an au pair this summer?**

We're a friendly American family with two children. We live in Madrid, Spain.

– Contact Lisa Jones for more information. –

Can he/she …	Emily	Ben
cook?		
drive?		
speak Spanish?		
play tennis?		
swim?		
play the piano?		
play the guitar?		
sing?		

8 ▶5.7 In pairs, ask and answer the questions about Emily and Ben. Who is best for the job? Listen and check.

A *Can Emily cook?*   B *Yes, she can.*

Go to Communication practice: Student A page 137, Student B page 145

9 A Ask your classmates questions 1–5. Find someone who says "Yes, I can." and write his/her name. Then ask for more information.
A *Can you speak a foreign language?*   B *Yes, I can.*
A *Which language can you speak?*   B *I can speak French.*

Questions	Name	More information
1 Can you speak a foreign language?		
2 Can you play an instrument?		
3 Can you dance?		
4 Can you cook?		
5 Can you play any sports?		

B In pairs, discuss what you found out about your classmates.

Sebastian can speak French.

Personal Best Write ten sentences about people in your class. Use *can* and *can't*.

5 SKILLS

LISTENING — listening for specific information ■ sentence stress ■ electronic devices

5B I can't live without my phone

1 Match the words in the box with the electronic devices 1–6. Is your family like this?

headphones   laptop   smartphone   mp3 player   TV   remote control

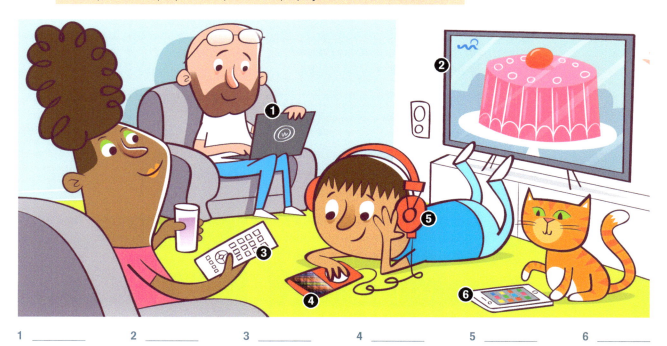

1 _____   2 _____   3 _____   4 _____   5 _____   6 _____

Go to Vocabulary practice: electronic devices, page 118

2 Which electronic devices do you have? Discuss in pairs.

I have a laptop, but I don't have a tablet.

3 ▶ 5.9   Watch or listen to the first part of *Learning Curve*. Check (✓) the devices Kate mentions.

camera ☐   desktop computer ☐   TV ☐   smartphone ☐   laptop ☐   headphones ☐

🛠 Skill   listening for specific information

We sometimes need to listen for specific information.
- Read the questions to find out what information you need.
- Think about the topic and what type of information it is, e.g., a person, a place, or a number.
- Listen carefully when the speakers talk about this topic.

4 ▶ 5.9   Read the Skill box. Watch or listen again, and choose the correct options to answer the questions.

1 Which sport does Kate play on Friday?
   a basketball   b soccer   c tennis
2 What language does she learn on her tablet and phone?
   a Spanish   b French   c Italian
3 What device can't she live without?
   a tablet   b camera   c phone
4 How many photos do people take every year?
   a one million   b one billion   c one trillion
5 How many televisions do people in the U.S. have?
   a 116 million   b 123 million   c 26 million

listening for specific information ■ sentence stress ■ electronic devices   **LISTENING**   **SKILLS 5B**

5 ▶ **5.10** Watch or listen to the rest of the show. Complete the sentences with the words in the box.

headphones   DVR   car   laptop   tablet   music

1 Simon can't live without _____ or his _____ .

2 Parminder can't live without her _____ and _____ .

3 Vincent can't live without his _____ and his _____ .

6 ▶ **5.10** Watch or listen again. Choose the correct options to complete the sentences.
1 Parminder uses her devices for *presentations / letters / games*.
2 She uses her devices *on the weekend / at night / every day*.
3 Vincent can play *the piano / the violin / the guitar*.
4 His car is from *1962 / 1967 / 1972*.
5 Simon travels *by underground / on foot / by car*.

7 ▶ **5.11** Listen to Vincent's sentence. Is it easy to hear the underlined words? Why?

> And when I <u>get</u> home, I <u>watch</u> TV at night.

Listening builder   sentence stress

In English, we stress the important words in sentences. You can usually understand the general idea if you only hear these words.

I <u>play</u> <u>basketball</u> on <u>Fridays</u> with a <u>women's</u> <u>team</u>.
I <u>work</u> for a <u>big</u> <u>company</u>, and we <u>use</u> <u>all</u> the <u>top</u> <u>technology</u>.

8 A ▶ **5.12** Read the Listening builder. Read and listen to sentences 1–4. Can you understand them?
1 _____ can't live without _____ phone. _____ _____ call people _____ take photos.
2 _____ brother's _____ doctor. _____ usually goes _____ _____ hospital _____ car.
3 Kevin wants _____ new laptop, _____ _____ very expensive.
4 _____ _____ morning, _____ always listen _____ _____ radio.

B ▶ **5.12** Listen again and complete the sentences with the unstressed words.

9 In pairs, talk about your electronic devices. Answer the questions.
1 What do you use your devices for?
2 Which device can't you live without? Why not?
A *I use my phone to listen to music and take photos. What about you?*
B *I don't use my phone to take photos. I have a good camera.*

Personal Best   Write about your favorite electronic device. Say when and where you use it.

5 LANGUAGE — object pronouns ■ activities

5C I love it!

1 Match the words in the box with pictures a–f.

> bike riding   walking   cleaning   swimming   reading   cooking

Go to Vocabulary practice: activities, page 119

2 A Write two activities in each column.

😊 I love …	🙂 I like …	🙁 I don't like …	😔 I hate …

B Tell your partner about what you love, like, don't like, and hate.

A *I love cooking.*   **B** *Really? I hate cooking. I love going out!*

3 A Look at the pictures on the webpage. What activities can you see?

B Read the text. Complete the sentences with *loves*, *likes*, *doesn't like*, and *hates*.

1 Midori _____ listening to music. She _____ Taylor Swift.
2 Laura _____ grocery shopping.
3 Diego _____ visiting his grandpa.
4 Josh _____ sleeping late because he _____ early mornings.
5 Ellie _____ watching movies with her friends, and she _____ popcorn.

That's interesting — LIKES AND DISLIKES

I like listening to music. Taylor Swift is my favorite singer. I love her!
♥ 4   **Midori**

I like watching movies with my friends. We always have a big bowl of popcorn – I love it!
♥ 6   **Ellie**

My brother and I don't like grocery shopping. Mom always takes us on the weekend!
♥ 7   **Laura**

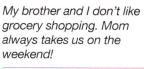

I love visiting my grandpa. I can always talk to him, and he helps me a lot.
♥ 12   **Diego**

I love sleeping late on weekends. Early mornings? I hate them!
♥ 3   **Josh**

object pronouns ■ activities   LANGUAGE 5C

4 A Match the object pronouns in **bold** with the people and things. Read the text again and check.

1 I love **her**!
2 Mom always takes **us** on the weekend!
3 I can always talk to **him**.
4 He helps **me** a lot.
5 I hate **them**!
6 I love **it**!

a Diego
b early mornings
c Taylor Swift
d popcorn
e Laura and her brother
f Diego's grandpa

B Choose the correct words to complete the sentences. Then read the Grammar box.

1 We use object pronouns instead of *people and things / times and places*.
2 We use object pronouns *before / after* verbs.

Grammar object pronouns

Subject pronouns:	Object pronouns:	
I	me	*I* don't understand. Can you help **me**?
you	you	Are **you** Adam? This is for **you**.
he	him	*He* isn't friendly. I don't like **him**.
she	her	*She* works in your office. Do you know **her**?
it	it	*It*'s perfect. I love **it**!
we	us	*We*'re in the yard. Can you see **us**?
they	them	*They*'re new here. I don't know **them**.

Go to Grammar practice: object pronouns, page 100

5 A ▶ 5.15 **Pronunciation:** the /h/ sound Listen and repeat. Pay attention to the /h/ sound.

him   her   he   help   happy

B ▶ 5.16 Say the questions and sentences. Then listen, check, and repeat.

1 Do you like him?   2 I can't see her.   3 He hates horses.   4 Hi, Harry. How are you?

6 ▶ 5.17 Complete the conversation with object pronouns. Listen and check.

A Do you like Emma Stone?
B Yes, I do. I love ¹_____ . She's great!
A What about Bruno Mars?
B Yes, I like ²_____ too.
A Do you like shopping for clothes?

B No, I hate ³_____ .
A Do you like Monday mornings?
B No, I hate ⁴_____ .
A What do you think of cats?
B I don't like ⁵_____ , but they like ⁶_____ !

Go to Communication practice: Student A page 138, Student B page 146

7 A Write three examples in each of the circles.

B In pairs, ask and answer questions about the people and things.

Do you like …?   What about …?   What do you think of …?

8 Tell the class about you and your partner.

We both love cats. I like Ryan Gosling, but Carla doesn't like him.

Personal Best Write a conversation like the one in exercise 6 between you and someone in your family.

47

5 SKILLS   WRITING   describing yourself ■ *because*

5D My profile

1 A Look at the profile on the "CityMeet" app. What do you think you can do with the app?
  a find an apartment in a city   b make new friends in a city   c find a new job in a city
B Read the profile and check.

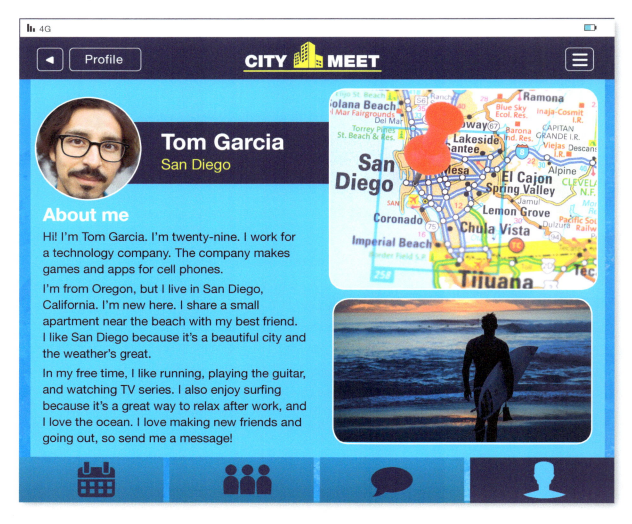

2 Read the profile again. Complete the sentences with the correct words.
  1 Tom works for a _____ company.
  2 He's from _____ , but he lives in _____ .
  3 He lives near the _____ with his _____ .
  4 He thinks the weather in San Diego is _____ .
  5 He plays the _____ and watches _____ in his free time.
  6 He loves making _____ .

Skill   describing yourself

When you write a text to describe yourself, use a different paragraph for each topic.
  • personal information about you and your job: *Hi! My name's Marta. I'm a teacher.*
  • where you live: *I live in Rio. I share an apartment with my best friend.*
  • what you do in your free time: *In my free time, I like listening to music and cooking for friends.*
  • information about your family: *I have a brother. His name's Paulo, and he's 18.*

3 Read the Skill box. Check (✓) the topics that are in Tom's profile.
  a his job ☐   b where he lives ☐   c his family ☐   d his free-time activities ☐

describing yourself ■ *because* **WRITING** **SKILLS** **5D**

4 Complete Kimberley's profile with sentences a–c.

a I also love traveling because it's a great way to meet new people.
b I study French and Spanish. I can also speak Portuguese.
c We love San Diego because it's a fun and exciting city.

ABOUT ME

Hello! I'm Kimberley Watson, and I'm a student at the University of San Diego. [1]____
I live in a house with four friends. We're all students. [2]____
In my free time, I like watching French movies, running, and going out with my friends. [3]____

5 Imagine Tom and Kimberley meet on CityMeet. Do they become friends? Choose an option and complete the sentence.

Tom and Kimberley *become / don't become* friends because _____ .

Text builder *because*

We use *because* to give a reason. It answers the question *Why?*
I like San Diego **because** *it's a beautiful city.*
Why do you like traveling? **Because** *it's a great way to meet new people.*

6 A Read the Text builder and find sentences with *because* in Tom and Kimberley's profiles. How do you say *because* in your language?

B Match 1–5 with a–e. Make sentences with *because*.

1 I live in a small apartment
2 I go to work by bus
3 I like swimming
4 I don't often go to the gym
5 I like living in a small town

a I'm usually tired after work.
b it's good exercise.
c it's quiet and the people are friendly.
d houses in the city are expensive.
e I can't drive.

7 Complete the sentences with your own ideas.

1 I love my city/town because _____ .
2 I'm often tired in the evening because _____ .
3 I like cooking because _____ .
4 I don't often go out because _____ .
5 I usually get up early because _____ .

8 A **PREPARE** Plan an online profile for you. Decide what information to include. Make notes about:

• your personal information
• your work or study
• where you live and who you live with
• your free-time activities and why you like them

B **PRACTICE** Write your profile. Use one paragraph for each topic. Remember to use *because* to give reasons.

C **PERSONAL BEST** Read your partner's profile. Does each paragraph contain one topic? Choose a paragraph that you like and tell your partner why you like it.

Personal Best Write a profile of a friend or someone in your family.

49

UNIT 6 Places

LANGUAGE — *there is/are* ■ places in town

6A City or town?

1 Match the words in the box with places 1–6.

bank   bus stop   restaurant
hotel   grocery store   post office

1 _____   3 _____   5 _____
2 _____   4 _____   6 _____

Go to Vocabulary practice: places in town, page 120

2 A Look at the pictures of Whycocomagh in Canada. Is it a city or a town?

B Read the text and check (✓) the things Whycocomagh has.

1 shopping mall ☐   3 movie theater ☐   5 school ☐
2 grocery store ☐   4 club ☐   6 restaurants ☐

An unusual job offer

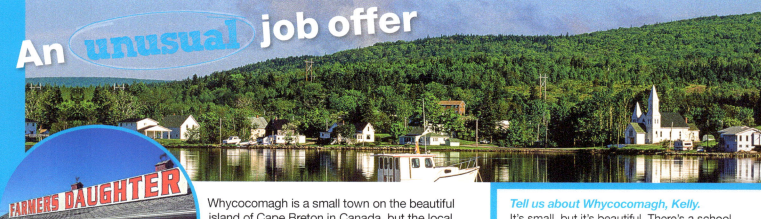

Whycocomagh is a small town on the beautiful island of Cape Breton in Canada, but the local grocery store has a problem. It needs three new salesclerks, and people don't want to come to live in Whycocomagh because it's very quiet and far from any big cities.

So the owners of the Farmer's Daughter store put an unusual job posting on Facebook. It says, *"We can't give you big money, but we can give you an awesome life"* … and they offer over 2,000 acres of free land!

Thousands of people from around the world are interested and want to work in the town, so now the grocery store has some new salesclerks. But what's the town really like? We talk to Kelly Jenkins, a teacher at the local school.

Tell us about Whycocomagh, Kelly.
It's small, but it's beautiful. There's a school, a post office, and the local grocery store, of course! There are also some hotels and restaurants for tourists.

Is there a shopping mall or a movie theater?
No, there's not! There aren't any big stores and there's no movie theater or clubs. But there are some wonderful people here. Everyone is very friendly.

Are there any problems?
Yes, there are … but life's boring without any problems!

3 Complete the sentences with the words in the box. Check your answers in the text.

's no   's   aren't   are (x2)   is

1 There _____ a school.
2 _____ there a shopping mall?
3 There _____ any big stores.
4 There _____ movie theater.
5 There _____ some wonderful people.
6 _____ there any problems?

50

there is/are ■ places in a town **LANGUAGE 6A**

4 Look at the sentences in exercise 3 again and choose the correct options to complete the rules. Then read the Grammar box.
1 We use *there's* and *there's no* with *singular / plural* nouns.
2 We use *there are* and *there are no* with *singular / plural* nouns.
3 We use *some / any* with plural nouns in affirmative sentences.
4 We use *some / any* with plural nouns in negative sentences and questions.

Grammar *there is/are*

Affirmative:
There's a movie theater.
There are some stores.

Negative:
There's no museum.
There aren't any cafés. /
There are no cafés.

Questions:
Is there a park?
Are there any hotels?

Short answers:
Yes, **there is**.   No, **there isn't**.
Yes, **there are**. No, **there aren't**.

Go to Grammar practice: *there is/are*, page 101

5 In pairs, say if you want to live in Whycocomagh. Explain your answers.
I don't want to live in Wycocomagh because there ...

6 ▶ 6.3 Complete the text with the correct form of *there is/are*. Listen and check.

This is the beautiful city of Lavasa in India. ¹_____ some nice apartments near the river. ²_____ a post office, a police station, and ³_____ also some great restaurants and cafés. ⁴_____ no train station, but if you need to travel by train, you can take a taxi to Pune, which is 60 kilometers away. However, ⁵_____ something strange about Lavasa … nobody lives here! ⁶_____ people in the apartments. On the weekend, ⁷_____ some tourists in the restaurants and hotels, but they're on vacation.

7 A ▶ 6.4 **Pronunciation:** linking consonants and vowels Listen and repeat the sentences from exercise 6. Pay attention to how the sounds link together.
1 There's‿a post‿office.
2 There's no‿train station.
3 There‿are no people.
4 There‿are some tourists.

B ▶ 6.5 Say the sentences linking the sounds together. Listen, check, and repeat.
1 There's‿a hospital.
2 Is there‿a bank?
3 There‿are some‿offices.
4 There‿are no‿museums.
5 There‿are some‿apartments.
6 Are there‿any old buildings?

Go to Communication practice: Student A page 138, Student B page 146

8 A ▶ 6.6 Listen to the conversation. Where does Erica live? Is she happy there?

B ▶ 6.6 Are the sentences about the area where Erica lives true (T) or false (F)? Listen again and check.
1 There's a big park.   ____
2 There's a movie theater.   ____
3 There are no stores.   ____
4 There's a café in her street. ____
5 There's no bus stop near her house. ____
6 There are some good restaurants. ____

9 Ask and answer the questions in pairs.

> Where do you live?   Is it a city or town?   What's your area like?
> Is there a …?   Are there any …?

Personal Best Write about a city or town you know well.

6 SKILLS READING reading in detail ■ giving opinions ■ parts of the body

6B City art

1 A Look at the pictures of public art on page 53. Do you like them? Why/Why not?

B Read the text quickly. In which cities can you see the three pieces of art?

Skill reading in detail

We sometimes have to read part of a text in detail to understand it well.
- Read the question and find the paragraph of the text that has the information you need.
- Read the paragraph very carefully to answer the question.
- We sometimes use different words and phrases to give the same information.

2 Read the Skill box. Choose the correct options to complete the sentences. Underline the phrase in the text that helped you answer the questions.

1 Carla and Mason have _____ .
  a jobs at the same hotel   b lots of cameras   c different opinions about *Eye*
2 Bruno Catalano _____ .
  a makes sculptures   b only has one arm   c is from Spain
3 Elodie and Christine _____ .
  a are friends of the artist   b live in Marseille   c are on vacation
4 Günther _____ the lifesaver fountain.
  a likes   b doesn't like   c doesn't give an opinion about
5 Helga works _____ .
  a in a school   b in a restaurant   c as a taxi driver

3 Match the words in the box with parts of the body 1–7 in the pictures on page 53.

head foot eye body leg hand arm

1 _____ 2 _____ 3 _____ 4 _____ 5 _____ 6 _____ 7 _____

Go to Vocabulary practice: parts of the body, page 121

4 Match the people with the opinions.

1 Carla   a "I don't think it means anything."
2 Mason   b "I like it."
3 Elodie and Christine   c "I think this is really ugly."
4 Günther   d "In my opinion, that's what it means."
5 Helga   e "It's beautiful."

Text builder giving opinions

Phrases: *In my opinion, ...   In my view, ...*
Verbs: *I think/don't think ...   I like/don't like ...*
Adjectives: *It's beautiful/ugly/interesting/boring/strange*, etc.

Look! We say: *I don't think it's ugly.*
NOT ~~I think it isn't ugly.~~

5 Read the Text builder. In pairs, describe the sculptures in the pictures and give your opinions.

a

b

c

reading in detail ■ giving opinions ■ parts of the body   **READING**   SKILLS   6B

I love it ...
but what is it?

There's art everywhere in our towns, cities, and parks. Sometimes it's good, sometimes it's bad, but it's always interesting.

Eye
In the courtyard of a five-star hotel in Dallas, in Texas, there's a 32-foot-high eye, called *Eye*. "It's really interesting," says Carla, a receptionist at the hotel. "There are cameras everywhere today, watching us. In my opinion, that's what it means." Mason, a waiter from another hotel, doesn't agree. "I don't think it means anything," he says. "It's just an eye!"

Travelers
In Marseille, France, there's an amazing sculpture by the French artist Bruno Catalano. It's a man on a trip. He only has one arm and he has no body.
"It's beautiful," say Elodie and her friend Christine, tourists from Paris.
"Perhaps it means that when we leave a place, we leave a part of us behind."

Lifesaver fountain
This fountain in Duisburg in Germany is big and colorful. It has a person's legs, but a bird's head and feet. But what is it? And what do local people think? "I usually like modern art," says Günther, a taxi driver. "But I think this is really ugly." Helga, a teacher, disagrees. "I like it," she says. "I often have lunch in a restaurant on this street. When I see the fountain, I feel happy."

Personal Best   Write about a piece of art you know and give your opinion of it.   53

6 LANGUAGE — prepositions of place ■ rooms and furniture

6C An unusual home

1 Match the furniture in the box with pictures a–f.

refrigerator   table   bed   sofa   closet   chair

 a
 b
 c
 d
 e
 f

Go to Vocabulary practice: rooms and furniture, page 122

2 In pairs, describe a room in your house. Can your partner guess the room?

A *There are four chairs in this room.*
A *No, it's my living room!*
B *Is it your kitchen?*

3 Look at the picture. Guess where Kirsten lives. Read the text and check.

Life on the water

For college students, a room in an apartment or a house can be very expensive, but not for 20-year-old Kirsten Müller. Kirsten is a student at a business school in Berlin … and she lives on a boat! It's small, but it's home.
Kirsten is on the sofa in the living room. There's a small table in front of her. "I study here every night," she says. "And I eat here too." The kitchen has an electric stove, and next to it, there's a small refrigerator. Kirsten cooks all her meals on the boat. "It's perfect for me, but I can't invite lots of friends for dinner!" The bedroom has a bed … and nothing else! All of Kirsten's clothes are in boxes under the bed because there's no closet. Between the bedroom and the kitchen, there's a modern bathroom with a shower and a toilet.
Kirsten loves her home. It's cheap, and the people on the other boats are friendly, but are there any problems? "I don't like getting up in the winter," she says. "It's very cold!"

4 Read the text again. Match the rooms in the box with the parts of the boat.

living room   bathroom   bedroom   kitchen

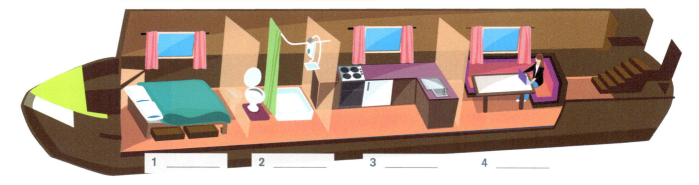

1 _____   2 _____   3 _____   4 _____

prepositions of place ■ rooms and furniture   LANGUAGE 6C

5 Look at the diagram in exercise 4 again. Complete the sentences with the prepositions of place in the box. Check your answers in the text. Then read the Grammar box.

under   between   in   on   next to   in front of

1 Kirsten is _____ the sofa.
2 There's a small table _____ her.
3 The kitchen has an electric stove, and _____ it, there's a small refrigerator.
4 All of Kirsten's clothes are _____ boxes _____ the bed.
5 _____ the bedroom and the kitchen, there's a modern bathroom.

Grammar   prepositions of place

There's a table **next to** the sofa.
My cell phone is **in** my purse.
Your shoes are **under** the bed.
My keys are **on** the table.

My bedroom is **above** our living room.
Luca sits **between** Carlos and Emma.
Your car is **in front of** our house.
The cat is **behind** the sofa.

Go to Grammar practice: prepositions of place, page 101

6 ▶ 6.10 **Pronunciation:** sentence stress Listen and repeat the sentences. Pay attention to the underlined stressed words.

1 The camera is under my bed.
2 Your head is in front of the TV.
3 His shoes are next to the sofa.
4 The bathroom is behind the door.

7 A Complete the sentences with the correct prepositions of place.

1 The window is _____ the table.
2 Your keys are _____ the book.
3 The books are _____ the shelves.
4 There's a bed _____ the window and the chair.

B ▶ 6.11 In pairs, say the sentences with the correct stress. Listen, check, and repeat.

8 A ▶ 6.12 Look at the picture and listen to the description. Find six differences between the description and the picture.

B ▶ 6.12 Compare your answers in pairs. Listen again and check.

There's no clock on the table. There's a lamp on the table.

Go to Communication practice: Student A page 138, Student B page 146

9 A Think of a room in your house. Make notes about what furniture is in it and where it is.

B In pairs, describe your room. Your partner draws it. Then check your pictures.

10 Ask and answer the questions in pairs.
1 Do you live in a house or an apartment?
2 Which is your favorite room? Why?
3 Imagine your ideal bedroom/living room/kitchen. What's in it?

Personal Best   Write about your "dream" home.

55

6 SKILLS SPEAKING checking information ■ asking for and giving directions

6D Is there a post office near here?

1 In pairs, discuss what you usually do when you're lost.
   a Ask someone in the street for directions.
   b Go into a store and ask for directions.
   c Look at a map.
   d Use a GPS app on your phone.
   e Walk around and hope you find the place.

2 6.13 Watch or listen to the first part of *Learning Curve*. Choose the correct words to complete the sentences.
   1 Simon has *cereal and tea / eggs, toast, and coffee / eggs, toast, and tea* for breakfast.
   2 He never goes to work *by car / by bike / on the subway*.
   3 Kate always says *"the underground" / "the subway" / "the tube."*
   4 The man wants to find *a parking lot / a post office / the subway station*.

3 6.13 Complete the conversation with phrases a–e. Watch or listen again, and check.

   Man   Excuse me. ¹_____
   Simon Yes, there is. ²_____
            Go straight on. ³_____
   Man   ⁴_____
   Simon ⁵_____

   a It's on the left, near the car park.
   b Thank you very much.
   c No problem.
   d It's down the street.
   e Is there a post office around here?

Conversation builder — asking for and giving directions

Asking for directions:
Excuse me.
Is there a post office near here?
Is there a post office around here?
Where's the post office?

Giving directions:
Go straight on/ahead.
Go down this street.
Turn right/left at …
It's on the right/left/corner.
It's near/next to/across from …

4 A Read the Conversation builder. In pairs, look at the maps, and ask for and give directions to the orange places.
   A *Excuse me, where's the bank?*   **B** *Go straight ahead …*

B 6.14 Listen and check. Are your conversations similar?

checking information ■ asking for and giving directions **SPEAKING**   SKILLS **6D**

5 ▶ 6.15 Watch or listen to the second part of the show. Choose the correct options to answer the questions.

1 Where do the women want to go?
   a To the movie theater.
   b To the shopping center.
   c To the grocery store.

2 What's the problem at the studio?
   a There's no water.
   b There's no tea.
   c There's no electricity.

6 ▶ 6.15 Watch or listen again. Complete the conversations with the phrases in the box.

> a problem   show me   near here   did you say   repeat that   you mean

1 **Woman 1** Is there a shopping center ¹_____?
  Simon Yes, it's near the supermarket. Go down this street, turn right on Bethnal Green Road. Don't stop at Ebor Street. Go straight ahead.
  Woman 2 I'm sorry, ²_____ near the supermarket?

2 **Woman 1** Can you ³_____ on the map?
  Simon We're here. And there's the cinema. And there's the supermarket. The shopping center is next to the supermarket. See?
  Woman 2 Could you ⁴_____, please? More slowly.

3 **Kate** There's ⁵_____, so there's no water in the kitchen or the bathroom. But there's water under the receptionist's desk! Poor Marina.
  Simon I'm sorry, did you say there's a problem on the street? ⁶_____, a problem with the water?

Skill — checking information

If you don't understand what someone says, you can:
- ask him/her to repeat: *Could you repeat that, please?   Could you say that again?*
- ask him/her to speak more slowly: *Could you speak more slowly, please?*
- ask a question to check the information: *Did you say near the supermarket?   You mean, a problem with the water?*

7 A ▶ 6.16 Read the Skill box. Listen and match phrases a–d with conversations 1–4. Where are the people in the situations?

a I'm sorry, did you say …? _____
b I'm sorry, could you say that again, please? _____
c I'm sorry, could you repeat that, please? _____
d I'm sorry, could you speak more slowly, please? _____

B ▶ 6.16 Listen again and complete the information that the people repeat.

1 Turn right at the _____.
  Then turn _____ at the _____.
2 _____ . _____ @mail.com
3 708 _____
4 $ _____

Go to Communication practice: Student A page 139, Student B page 147

8 A PREPARE In pairs, think of four places in your town. Think about how to get to the places from where you are now.

> a train station or bus stop
> a restaurant or café
> a museum or tourist attraction
> a shopping mall or grocery store

B PRACTICE Ask for and give directions. Check the information if you don't understand something.

C PERSONAL BEST Swap partners and ask for and give directions to a new place. Are you more confident asking for directions in English?

Personal Best Write an e-mail to a friend with directions to your house from the bus or train station.

57

5 and 6 REVIEW and PRACTICE

Grammar

1 Choose the correct options to complete the sentences.

1 On Saturdays, I meet my friends _____ the shopping mall.
   a on   b under   c at

2 _____ shelves in the living room.
   a There are no
   b There
   c There's no

3 He can't _____ coffee. It's always horrible!
   a make   b to make   c makes

4 My friends live in the city. I meet _____ on the weekend.
   a they   b them   c us

5 There are _____ in the kitchen.
   a any cookies
   b some cookie
   c some cookies

6 Your sunglasses are _____ to my laptop.
   a on   b in front   c next

7 A Is there a hospital in your town?
   B Yes, _____ .
   a there's
   b there is
   c there are

8 _____ drive a truck?
   a Do you can
   b Can you
   c You can

2 Complete the conversations with the words in the box.

| are no | any | can | can't | her |
| 's no | it | next to | on | them |

1 A _____ you swim?
   B Yes, I can, but there _____ swimming pool in this town.

2 A Are there _____ restaurants near here?
   B Yes, there's an Italian restaurant _____ the grocery store on School Street.

3 A Where are my headphones? I want to use _____ .
   B They're _____ the desk.

4 A Who can speak Spanish? I _____ read this menu.
   B Give _____ to me. I know some Spanish.

5 A Selina's class is at 8:00 p.m., but there _____ buses in the evening.
   B It's OK. I can drive _____ to the class.

3 Choose the correct options to complete the text.

A treehouse with a difference

If you want an unusual house, Jono Williams can [1] *make / makes* one for you. He's an engineer, and he loves treehouses, but his new Skysphere is different – it's very small, and it's not [2] *in / under* a tree!

What's in the Skysphere?
[3] *There's / There are* a large bed, a TV, and [4] *any / some* shelves. There's even a refrigerator for drinks [5] *between / in* the sofa! The windows are very large, and Jono [6] *can / can't* see 360° around the house. There's Wi-Fi, and he can [7] *use / using* his smartphone to play music and change the lights.

What does Jono do there?
Jono meets his friends at the Skysphere. They love [8] *them / it* too. They like listening to music, and at night they can watch the stars.

Are there [9] *some / any* **problems with Jono's house?**
Only one … there [10] *'s no / are no* bathroom.

Vocabulary

1 Put the words in the box in the correct columns.

| museum lamp table DVD player remote control |
| head teeth park chair GPS laptop desk |
| police station post office face foot |

Places in town	Electronic devices	Parts of the body	Furniture

REVIEW and PRACTICE 5 and 6

2 (Circle) the word that is different. Explain your answers.

1 sink	bathtub	table	shower
2 ear	mouth	nose	hand
3 school	grocery store	restaurant	café
4 bank	kitchen	bedroom	living room
5 chair	arm	refrigerator	closet
6 walking	reading	swimming	bike riding
7 sing	speak	travel	call
8 DVD player	shelves	computer	GPS

3 Choose the correct options to complete the sentences.

1 My city has two _____ .
   a closets   b hospitals   c bathrooms

2 What time does the bus _____ downtown?
   a arrive   b travel   c go out

3 Her _____ is long and brown.
   a eye   b hair   c mouth

4 There's a large _____ in the living room.
   a bathtub   b leg   c sofa

5 She always uses _____ to listen to music on the bus.
   a earphones   b TV   c shelves

6 A Where's the _____ ?   B It's in the car.
   a museum   b bathroom   c GPS

7 Is there any cheese in the _____ ?
   a shower   b refrigerator   c DVR

8 On the weekend, I like _____ at the movie theater.
   a dancing   b sleeping   c watching movies

4 Complete the conversations with the words in the boxes.

> bedroom stove windows desk club cooking

Ama Hi, Ed! How are you? Do you like your new apartment?

Ed No, not really. It's above a noisy ⁱ_____ .

Ama Oh no! Is it big?

Ed No, it's very small. In the ²_____ , there's only a bed and a ³_____ , and there are no ⁴_____ in the bathroom.

Ama How's the kitchen? I know you like ⁵_____ .

Ed It's dirty and the ⁶_____ is very old ... but it's a good apartment.

Ama What's good about it?

Ed It's cheap!

> call station office speak drive stop

Sam Excuse me. Do you ⁷_____ English?

Fran Yes, I do.

Sam Where's the bus ⁸_____ ?

Fran It's in front of the post ⁹_____ , but there are no buses today.

Sam OK. Is there a train ¹⁰_____ near here?

Fran Yes, but it's a long walk. I can ¹¹_____ you there if you want.

Sam No thanks, I can ¹²_____ a taxi.

Personal Best

Lesson 5A
Write one affirmative and one negative sentence about your abilities.

Lesson 6A
Name five places in your town.

Lesson 5B
Name four electronic devices that you use.

Lesson 6A
Write three questions to find out what there is in a friend's town.

Lesson 5C
Name two activities that you like doing and two activities that you don't like doing.

Lesson 6B
Write your opinion of a famous building.

Lesson 5C
Write four sentences with different object pronouns.

Lesson 6B
Name five parts of the body that you have two of.

Lesson 5D
Write four sentences to describe yourself.

Lesson 6C
Name four things in your house and describe where they are.

Lesson 5D
Say why you like/don't like your town/city using *because*.

Lesson 6D
Write directions from the classroom to a store, café, school, or bus stop.

59

UNIT 7 All in the past

LANGUAGE simple past: *be* ■ celebrities

7A When they were young

1 Match the jobs in the box with pictures a–f.

musician   politician   movie director   writer   soccer player   fashion model

Go to Vocabulary practice: celebrities, page 123

2 In pairs, describe celebrities. Can your partner guess who it is?

A *She's a tennis player. She's American. She's very good!*   **B** *Is it Serena Williams?*

3 A Read the introduction of the text. Match the blue sign with one of the people a–e.

B Read the rest of the text. Match the other people with descriptions 1-4. Check their names on page 139 and write their names on the blue signs.

London's famous houses

London was home to lots of famous people from all over the world. Who were they and where were their houses? It's easy – just look for the blue signs on the buildings!

1869–1948 Lived here as a law student

1 He was a famous Indian politician, but he was also a student in London for three years. He was a vegetarian, and, in the 19th century, it wasn't easy to find good vegetarian food in the city.

1945–1981 Singer and musician Lived here 1972

2 In 1972, London was home to this Jamaican singer and his band. The musicians weren't famous then, but a year later their song *Stir It Up* was a big hit.

1890–1976 Writer Lived here 1934–1941

3 This British writer wasn't from London, but she was here for seven years. Her crime stories were very popular around the world, and you probably know her famous detective – Hercule Poirot.

1853–1890 Artist Lived here 1873–1874

4 This was the Dutch artist's home when he was 19 years old. He was in love with the owner's daughter, Eugenie. But was she interested in him? No, she wasn't!

simple past: *be* ■ celebrities   **LANGUAGE**   **7A**

4 A Complete the sentences with the words in the box. Check your answers in the text.

was (x2)   were (x2)   wasn't   weren't

1 Where _____ their houses?
2 He _____ a famous Indian politician.
3 It _____ easy to find good vegetarian food.
4 The musicians _____ famous then.
5 Her crime stories _____ very popular.
6 _____ she interested in him?

B Complete the rules. Then read the Grammar box.

1 The simple past forms of *is*/*'s not* = _____ / _____ .
2 The simple past forms of *are*/*'re not* = _____ / _____ .

Grammar   simple past: *be*

Affirmative:	Negative:	Questions:	Short answers:	
He **was** a musician.	I **wasn't** an actor.	**Was** she a writer?	Yes, she **was**.	No, she **wasn't**.
They **were** singers.	You **weren't** famous.	**Were** you happy?	Yes, we **were**.	No, we **weren't**.

Go to Grammar practice: simple past: *be*, page 102

5 A ▶ 7.3   **Pronunciation:** *was/were* Listen and repeat the question and answer.
How are *was* and *were* pronounced?

A *Where were you yesterday?*   B *I was at work.*

B In pairs, ask and answer the question *Where were you …?* with the times in the boxes.
Pay attention to the pronunciation of *was* and *were*.

A *Where were you at 7:30 this morning?*   B *I was on the bus. I always go to work early. What about you?*
A *I was in bed!*

at 7:30 this morning   yesterday morning   yesterday at 2:00 p.m.   yesterday evening

Go to Communication practice: Student A page 139, Student B page 147

6 ▶ 7.4   Complete the sentences with the correct form of *was* or *were*. Listen and check.

When they were young

- Singer Justin Timberlake and actor Ryan Gosling [1]_____ hosts on a children's TV show when they [2]_____ young.

- In 1990, J.K. Rowling [3]_____ an English teacher in Portugal, but she [4]_____ happy there. Seven years later, she [5]_____ famous all over the world as the writer of the *Harry Potter* books.

- Actors and movie directors Matt Damon and Ben Affleck [6]_____ in school together, but they [7]_____ in the same class.

- Athlete Usain Bolt [8]_____ interested in cricket and soccer in school. His teachers [9]_____ surprised because he [10]_____ a very, very fast runner!

7 In pairs, ask and answer questions about when you were young. Use the ideas below.

A *What was the name of your first teacher?*   B *Mrs. Fuentes. She was really nice. What about you?*

1 What / the name of your first teacher?
2 / you a good student?
3 / you in a big class?
4 Who / your best friend?
5 What celebrities / popular when you / a child?
6 What movies / popular?
7 What / your favorite TV shows?
8 What / your favorite food?

Personal Best   Think of someone famous that you like. Write a paragraph about their life when they were young.

7 SKILLS LISTENING — listening for dates ■ linking consonants and vowels ■ months and ordinals

7B I was there in July

1 Order the months from 1–12.

- ☐ April
- ☐ August
- ☐ December
- ☐ February
- ☒ January (1)
- ☐ July
- ☐ June
- ☐ March
- ☐ May
- ☐ November
- ☐ October
- ☐ September

May calendar

May						
1 a	2	3 b	4	5	6	7
8	9	10	11	12 c	13	14
15	16	17	18	19	20 d	21
22	23	24	25	26	27	28 e
29	30	31 f				

2 Look at the calendar. Match days a–f with dates 1–6.

1 May thirty-first _____
2 May twentieth _____
3 May twenty-eighth _____
4 May twelfth _____
5 May first _____
6 May third _____

Go to Vocabulary practice: months and ordinals, page 124

3 Ask and answer the questions in pairs.

1 What's the date today?
2 When's your birthday?
3 What's your favorite month?
4 When was the last national holiday?

4 A Look at the picture. What do you know about Shakespeare?

B Complete the text with the words in the box.

> April   *Hamlet*   plays   writer

William Shakespeare was a famous British ¹_____ . He was born on ²_____ 26, 1564, and he died in April, 1616. His ³_____ are popular all over the world. They include *Romeo and Juliet*, ⁴_____ , and *Othello*.

5 ▶ 7.7 Watch or listen to the first part of *Learning Curve*. Are the sentences true (T) or false (F)?

1 Shakespeare's plays are only about British people. _____
2 The Globe Theatre was Shakespeare's first theater. _____
3 "Shakespeare in the Park" in New York is very expensive. _____
4 You can read Shakespeare's plays in 80 different languages. _____

🔧 Skill   listening for dates

It's sometimes important to listen for specific years and months.

- Listen carefully because some months sound similar: *September, November* and *December*.
- Years are usually divided into two numbers: *1990 = nineteen ninety, 2010 = twenty ten*.
  For years after 2000, we sometimes use the whole number: *2009 = two thousand and nine*.
- We use ordinals to talk about centuries (100 years): *1900–1999 = the twentieth century*.

6 ▶ 7.7 Read the Skill box. Watch or listen again. Complete the texts with the correct information.

> The Globe Theatre was Shakespeare's first theater. It was here in London during the ¹_____ and ²_____ centuries, from ³_____ to about ⁴_____ . This theater looks just like the old Globe.
>
> Every year, from ⁵_____ to ⁶_____ , there's a Shakespeare festival in Central Park in New York City. It's called "Shakespeare in the Park." 1,800 people can see a Shakespeare play at the Delacorte Theater for free!

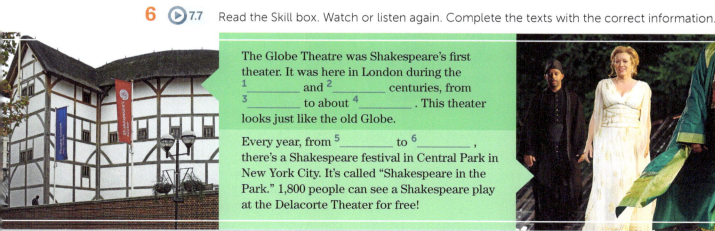

listening for dates ■ linking consonants and vowels ■ months and ordinals **LISTENING** **SKILLS** **7B**

7 ▶ 7.8 Watch or listen to the rest of the show. Match the people with sentences 1–4.

Marty

Elizabeth and Henry

Zhang

1 This person likes plays about love. _____
2 This person works at a theater. _____
3 This person doesn't like Shakespeare. _____
4 This person likes plays about history. _____

8 ▶ 7.8 Watch or listen again. Answer the questions with months or years.
1 When does Marty come to New York? _____ and _____
2 When were Elizabeth and Henry in Cambridge? _____
3 When was *A Midsummer Night's Dream* in Beijing? _____
4 When was *Henry IV* at the Hong Kong Arts Festival? _____

9 Ask and answer the questions in pairs.

> Do you ever go to the theater?
> Which Shakespeare plays do you know?
> Which types of plays do you like?
> Do you like Shakespeare? Why/Why not?

10 ▶ 7.9 Listen to Penny's sentence and look at the linked words. Pay attention to how the sounds join together.

> A lot‿of people‿are here‿in the line for theater tickets.

| **Listening builder** | linking consonants and vowels |

When a word ends in a consonant sound, and the next word starts with a vowel sound, we usually link the sounds together.
Hamlet‿is‿about‿a prince‿in Denmark.
I'm‿Elizabeth,‿and this‿is my husband, Henry.
Sometimes the plays‿are‿in‿English‿and Chinese.

11 ▶ 7.10 Read the Listening builder. Then listen and complete the sentences.
1 Hi, my name's Lucas, _____ _____ _____ _____ .
2 In _____ _____ _____ _____ New York City for the first time.
3 The play _____ _____ _____ _____ king.
4 She was born on _____ _____ _____ , 1999.
5 I like *Hamlet*, but I _____ _____ _____ the story.

12 Look at the pictures. Discuss the questions in pairs.

1 When was the last time you were at a play/a movie theater/a concert?
2 Which play/movie/band was it?
3 Was it good? Why/Why not?

Personal Best Write a description of your favorite play or movie. Where does it happen? What's it about?

7 LANGUAGE — simple past: regular verbs ■ time expressions

7C Famous decades

1 Match the decades in the box with a–f.

the nineties   the twenty-tens   the seventies   the two-thousands   the sixties   the eighties

a  b  c  d  e  f

2 Discuss the questions in pairs.

I was born in the eighties. What about you?

1 In which decade were you born?
2 Which decade has the best music and fashion, in your opinion?
3 Which was your favorite decade? Why?

3 ▶ 7.11 In pairs, complete the quiz with the years in the box. Listen and check.

1969   1973   1985   1991   2004   2012

The Decades Quiz

On February 4, ¹_____ , Mark Zuckerberg started Facebook from his bedroom in college. He wanted 500 people to join. Now, more than 1.5 billion people use it!

In ⁴_____ , Korean singer PSY danced *Gangnam Style* all over the world. The song was number 1 in 37 countries. Did you watch the video?

On July 20, ²_____ , Neil Armstrong and Buzz Aldrin walked on the moon. 600 million people watched on TV or listened on the radio.

On November 30, ⁵_____ , the U.S. and Norway played in the first Women's Soccer World Cup final in China. The result was a 2–1 win for the U.S.

In April ³_____ , Coca-Cola® tried a new recipe for their drink. People didn't like the flavor, and three months later, the original Coca-Cola was back in stores.

On April 3, ⁶_____ , Martin Cooper from Motorola called Joel Engel on the world's first cell phone. Joel quickly stopped the call because he wasn't happy. He worked for rival company AT&T!

4 Read the quiz again. Write the simple past form of verbs 1–8.

1 start _____   3 watch _____   5 dance _____   7 call _____
2 walk _____   4 try _____   6 play _____   8 stop _____

5 A Look at the verbs in exercise 4 again and complete the rules.

1 We usually add the letters ____ to verbs to make the simple past form.
2 If the verb ends in -e, we add the letter ____ to make the simple past form.
3 If the verb ends in consonant + y, we remove the y and add the letters ____ to make the simple past form.
4 If the verb ends in consonant + vowel + consonant, we double the last consonant and add ____.

B Complete the sentences from the text to make the negative and question forms of the simple past. Does the main verb change form? Read the Grammar box.

1 People _____ like the flavor.
2 _____ you watch the video?

simple past: regular verbs ■ time expressions

LANGUAGE 7C

Grammar simple past: regular verbs

Affirmative:
600 million people **watched** on TV.
Coca-Cola **tried** a new recipe.

Negative:
They **didn't call** on a smartphone.
Brazil **didn't play** in the final.

Questions and short answers:
Did you **try** the new drink?
Yes, I **did**.   No, I **didn't**.

Go to Grammar practice: simple past: regular verbs, page 102

6 ▶ 7.13 Complete the text with the simple past form of the verbs in parentheses. Listen and check.

Were the nineties the best decade for movies?

My brother ¹_____ (study) movies in college, and he thinks the nineties were the best decade for movies. So last week, I ²_____ (decide) to watch the movie *Titanic* for the first time. It was in theaters 20 years ago, but I was only two then.
I ³_____ (love) it … but it's a sad story. It's about a real disaster that ⁴_____ (happen) in 1912 in the Atlantic Ocean. Thousands of people ⁵_____ (die) because the ship ⁶_____ (not carry) enough lifeboats.
After that, I ⁷_____ (want) to see more movies from the nineties. So, on the weekend, I ⁸_____ (watch) *Jurassic Park*, *Forrest Gump*, and *Pulp Fiction*. On Monday, it was *Toy Story*, and last night, I ⁹_____ (start) watching *The Matrix* … but I ¹⁰_____ (not finish) it because at 1:00 a.m.
I ¹¹_____ (need) to go to bed. My brother was right – movies from the nineties are amazing!

7 Complete the time expressions with the words in the box. Check your answers in the text in exercise 6.

in   ago   last (x2)   on (x2)   at

1 20 years _____	3 _____ 1912	5 _____ night	7 _____ 1:00 a.m.
2 _____ week	4 _____ the weekend	6 _____ Monday	

Go to Vocabulary practice: time expressions, page 124

8 A ▶ 7.15 **Pronunciation:** *-ed* endings Listen and repeat the sentences from the text.
Pay attention to the *-ed* endings in **bold**: /d/, /t/, and /ɪd/.

1 /d/   lov**ed**   I lov**ed** it.
2 /t/   watch**ed**   I watch**ed** *Jurassic Park*.
3 /ɪd/ need**ed**   I need**ed** to go to bed.

B ▶ 7.16 Write the verbs in the box in the correct columns. Listen, check, and repeat.

danced   wanted   played   tried   walked   visited

/d/	/t/	/ɪd/

Go to Communication practice: Student A page 139, Student B page 147

9 A In pairs, ask and answer the questions with the simple past form of the verbs. Write your partner's answers in the chart.

A *When did you last watch a movie on DVD?*
B *I watched a movie on DVD about a year ago.*

When did you last …	Answers
1 watch / a movie on DVD?	
2 study / for an exam?	
3 cook / chicken?	
4 play / a musical instrument?	
5 call / a friend on the phone?	

When was the last time you …	Answers
6 use / a computer?	
7 dance / with friends?	
8 relax / at home?	
9 talk / to a neighbor?	
10 listen / to the radio?	

B Tell the class about your partner.

Marco watched a movie on DVD about a year ago.

Personal Best Choose six different time expressions and write a true simple past sentence for each one.

7 SKILLS WRITING writing informal e-mails ■ sequencers

7D A weekend away

1 In pairs, order the pictures from 1–6 to make a story about Elena and her father's trip to Boston.

2 Read Elena's e-mail and check the order of the pictures in exercise 1.

To: Becky Stewart
Subject: My weekend

Hi Becky,

How are things? I hope you're well.

Did I tell you about last weekend? I visited my sister Hannah. She lives in Boston now. I wanted to go on my own … but Dad decided to come with me!

We traveled by train on Saturday. We arrived in Boston and Hannah was at the train station. In the afternoon, we explored the city. First, we walked around one of the universities. It was beautiful, but Dad stopped to take hundreds of pictures! Then we visited an art gallery. Dad studied every painting and looked at every sculpture – we were there for hours! After that, Hannah and I wanted to go shopping, but Dad wanted to visit a museum. It was so boring!

It was a disaster! This weekend, I want to stay at home, or go away without Dad!
See you soon.
Elena

3 A Read the e-mail again. Are the sentences true (T) or false (F)?

1. Elena and her dad traveled to Boston. ____
2. They stayed in Boston for a week. ____
3. Elena's dad didn't like the university. ____
4. They explored the university on foot. ____
5. They didn't stay in the art gallery for a long time. ____
6. Hannah and Elena didn't want to visit the museum. ____

B Look at the e-mail again and answer the questions. Then read the Skill box.

1. How does Elena start her e-mail?
2. How does she ask how her friend is?
3. How does she introduce her news?
4. How does she finish her e-mail?

Skill writing informal e-mails

We write informal e-mails to friends and people we know well.
- Start the e-mail in a friendly way: *Hi …, Hello …*
- Ask about the person: *How are you? How are things? I hope you're well.*
- Say why you are writing: *Did I tell you about …? I wanted to tell/ask you …*
- Finish the e-mail in a friendly way: *See you soon, Bye for now, See you later.*

writing informal e-mails ■ sequencers **WRITING** SKILLS **7D**

4 Complete the e-mail with the words in the box.

> hope   how   hello   tell   now

To: George Hawkins
Subject: Fantastic weekend

¹_____ George,
²_____ are you? I ³_____ you and the family are well.
I wanted to ⁴_____ you about last weekend. My daughter Elena and I traveled to Boston.
My other daughter, Hannah, moved there a few months ago, so we stayed with her.
On Saturday, we walked into town. First, we explored one of the universities. It was very interesting. Elena loved all the old buildings! Then we visited an art gallery. We were there for hours – the girls didn't want to leave! After that, we looked around the museum. I was pretty tired, but the girls really enjoyed it. It was a great weekend. I think Elena wants to do it again soon.
Bye for ⁵_____ .
Frank

5 Discuss the questions in pairs.
1 Who is Frank?
2 What differences are there between Frank and Elena's e-mails?
3 Do you enjoy visiting art galleries and museums? Why/Why not?

6 Order sentences a–c from 1–3. Check your answers in the e-mail in exercise 4.
a ☐ After that, we looked around the museum.
b ☐ First, we explored the university.
c ☐ Then we visited an art gallery.

Text builder   sequencers

We can show the order of events with *First*, *Then*, and *After that*:
First, we walked into town.   *Then* we visited the university.   *After that,* we explored the downtown area.

Look! We usually use a comma after *First* and *After that*.

7 Read the Text builder. Then write sentences in the simple past with sequencers.

First, we listened to some music. Then we cooked dinner ...

1 We / listen to / some music. We / cook / dinner. We / watch / a movie.
2 She / visit / her sister. She / call / her mom. She / talk to / her dad.
3 I / walk to / my friend's house. We / study / English together. We / play / soccer.

8 A **PREPARE** Think of a weekend when you were somewhere interesting. Make notes about what happened. Think about:

- where you traveled to
- how you traveled
- who was with you
- where you stayed
- the places that you visited
- if you enjoyed it

Use these regular verbs to help you:

> visit   travel   play   walk   watch   listen to   wait   love
> cook   explore   stay   talk   enjoy   need   want   try

B **PRACTICE** Write an e-mail to a friend about your weekend. Use the Skill box and Text builder to help you.

C **PERSONAL BEST** Exchange e-mails with your partner. Does your partner use the simple past correctly? Can you correct any mistakes?

Personal Best — Write about a day when you visited a lot of places, like Elena's day in Boston.

UNIT 8 Travel

LANGUAGE simple past: irregular verbs ■ travel verbs

8A Incredible trips

1 Complete the sentences with the verbs in the box.

get lost   book   fly   miss   ride   take

1 Some of my friends _____ motorcycles to work.

3 I sometimes _____ the bus because I get up late.

5 I never _____ because I don't like it!

2 I always _____ train tickets early to get a good price.

4 If I go out at night, I usually _____ a taxi home.

6 I often _____ in a new town.

Go to Vocabulary practice: travel verbs, page 125

2 In pairs, say the sentences in exercise 1. Decide if they are true or false for your partner.

A *Some of my friends ride motorcycles to work.*   B *False.*
A *You're right. All my friends drive to work.*

3 Look at the title and the picture. In pairs, guess what the story is about. Read the text and check.

Around the world *for love*

In January 2001, Ian Johnstone from Yorkshire in the UK went to work in Australia for a year, but his girlfriend Amy stayed at home. It was difficult to be so far away from her and after six months, Ian planned to visit her. He wanted to ask her to marry him, but he didn't tell her about his plans … it was a surprise visit!

Ian booked a flight, and in July he flew from Sydney to London, with a layover in Singapore. But he didn't know about Amy's plans. She also wanted to surprise Ian with a visit, and at that exact moment, she was also on a plane … to Australia!

When Ian arrived in London, he bought some flowers and took the train to Yorkshire. Amy wasn't at home, so Ian waited for her. At the same time, Amy arrived at Ian's apartment in Sydney. When his roommate told her that Ian was 17,000 kilometers miles away in England, Amy thought that it was a joke!

It wasn't possible for Ian or Amy to change their tickets, so they didn't see each other. But the story had a happy ending. Ian called Amy and asked her to marry him. And what did she say? She said "yes," of course!

simple past: irregular verbs ■ travel verbs   **LANGUAGE** — **8A**

4 Are the sentences true (T) or false (F)? Read the text again and check.

1 Ian went to Australia with Amy. _____
2 He wanted to see his girlfriend. _____
3 Amy lived in London. _____
4 She traveled to Australia to see Ian. _____
5 They changed their tickets. _____
6 Amy didn't want to marry Ian. _____

5 **A** Look at the simple past verbs in **bold** in the sentence from the text. Which verb is regular and which is irregular?

Ian **booked** a flight, and in July he **flew** from Sydney to London.

B Find the simple past form of the irregular verbs in the text. Then read the Grammar box.

1 go _____ 2 fly _____ 3 buy _____ 4 take _____ 5 think _____ 6 say _____

📖 **Grammar** **simple past: irregular verbs**

Affirmative:
Ian **went** to work in Australia.
He **flew** to London.
He **bought** some flowers.

Negative:
Ian **didn't go** to work in Singapore.
He **didn't fly** to Sydney.
He **didn't buy** chocolate.

Questions:
Did Ian **go** home?
Did he **fly** alone?
Did he **buy** a ring?

Short answers:
Yes, he **did**.
No, he **didn't**.

Personal Best

Go to Grammar practice: simple past: irregular verbs, page 103

6 Complete the text with the simple past form of the verbs in parentheses.

Around the world – on foot! 👣 👣 👣 👣
This is Jean Béliveau, a Canadian who walked around the world, through 64 countries in 11 years!

When ^{1}_____ he _____ (leave)?
Jean ^{2}_____ (leave) his home on August 18, 2000, and he ^{3}_____ (not get) home until 2011.
His wife, Luce, ^{4}_____ (not go) with him, but she ^{5}_____ (fly) to meet him eleven times.
Where ^{6}_____ he _____ (sleep)?
He ^{7}_____ (sleep) in people's homes, parks, schools, hospitals – and even in a police station!
People also ^{8}_____ (buy) him food and drink.
Why ^{9}_____ he _____ (do) it?
He ^{10}_____ (do) it because he wanted people to know about children's lives in other countries.

7 **A** ▶ 8.3 **Pronunciation:** irregular simple past verbs Listen and repeat the simple past verbs. Pay attention to the vowel sounds /ɑ/, /ɔ/ and /ow/.

1 /ɑ/ got lost 2 /ɔ/ bought thought 3 /ow/ rode drove

B ▶ 8.4 Underline the words in the sentences with the same vowel sounds. Listen, check, and repeat.

1 I got on the bus.
2 We all bought a ticket.
3 I rode home on my bike.
4 He lost his job.
5 She thought it was her ball.
6 She drove to my home.

Go to Communication practice: Student A page 140, Student B page 148

8 **A** ▶ 8.5 Read Leanne's plans for a vacation in California last summer. Then listen and correct the information with what really happened.

B In pairs, make sentences about Leanne's trip.

She didn't fly from Tampa. She flew from Orlando.

9 Think about a vacation or trip. In pairs, ask and answer the questions in the boxes.

My trip to California
July 24: fly from Tampa to San Diego
July 30: take bus to Los Angeles
August 5: sail to Catalina Island
August 10: take taxi to San Francisco and drive home
Activities: *eat local food, swim in the ocean, take pictures … fall in love?*

Where did you go? How did you travel? What did you do?
When did you go? Who did you go with? Did you have a good time?

Personal Best Write about your partner's vacation or trip from exercise 9.

8 SKILLS READING understanding the main idea ■ modifiers ■ weather and seasons

8B Crazy weather!

1 Match the weather phrases in the box with pictures a–d on page 71.

> It's cold.   It's sunny.   It's raining.   It's windy.

Go to Vocabulary practice: weather and seasons, page 126

2 In pairs, talk about the seasons in your country. Use *love/like/don't like/hate*.
I don't like the fall because it rains, and it's cold and windy.

Skill understanding the main idea

When you see a text for the first time, try to understand the main idea quickly.
- Look at the title and pictures.
- Read the first line of each paragraph.
- Use this information to understand what the text is about.

3 A Read the Skill box. Then read the title and the highlighted sentences on page 71. Check (✔) the main idea.

- a Robbie had lots of problems with transportation in Germany. ☐
- b Robbie went on vacation, and the weather changed a lot. ☐
- c Robbie was in Berlin in the summer, but it snowed all week. ☐
- d Robbie didn't like the weather in Germany, so he went to Ireland. ☐

B Read the whole text and check.

4 Are the sentences true (T) or false (F)? Read the text again and check.

1. Robbie went to Berlin with his girlfriend. ____
2. They had ice cream in Viktoria Park. ____
3. They waited for a train for three hours. ____
4. It rained at the Television Tower. ____
5. They didn't go to the concert because it snowed. ____
6. They arrived at the airport late and missed the flight. ____

5 Match the halves to make sentences from the text. Do the modifiers in **bold** come before or after the adjectives?

1. When we got off the plane, it was **very**
2. When we got to the park, it was **pretty**
3. And in the afternoon, it was **really**
4. The views were**n't very**

a cold.
b good.
c windy.
d hot and sunny.

Text builder modifiers

We use modifiers before an adjective to make the meaning stronger or less strong:

▼ really/very   It was **really** sunny. The movie was **very** exciting.
  pretty   The museum was **pretty** interesting.
  not very   The food was**n't very** good.

6 Read the Text builder. Then write sentences with the words and a modifier.
The weather today is very hot.

1. the weather today / hot
2. the *Star Wars* movies / exciting
3. I think English / difficult
4. public transportation in my country / expensive
5. my street / noisy
6. people in my city / friendly

7 In pairs, talk about your last trip or vacation. What was the weather like?
Last year, I visited Morocco. It was very hot and sunny in the day, and really cold at night.

understanding the main idea ■ modifiers ■ weather and seasons **READING** SKILLS **8B**

Travel news

Four Seasons In One Week

Robbie Irwin

Monday, March 12

My girlfriend and I arrived in Berlin today on vacation. We thought Germany was cold in March, so we only brought winter clothes, but we had a surprise. When we got off the plane, it was very hot and sunny! So, this afternoon, we went shopping and bought shorts and T-shirts and walked around downtown. I even had ice cream!

a

Wednesday, March 14

Today, we decided to visit Viktoria Park, but the weather changed. It was warm when we left the hotel, so we wore our new shorts and T-shirts. But when we got to the park, it was pretty cold. And in the afternoon, it was really windy. We decided to visit Museum Island, so we took a train back into the city … but a tree fell on the tracks, and we didn't move for three hours! After that, we went back to the hotel, changed our clothes, and had dinner in a restaurant.

b

Thursday, March 15

The weather here is crazy – this morning it was sunny again! We decided to visit the famous Television Tower. It's over a thousand feet high and I wanted to take some pictures of the city. But when we got to the top of the tower, it was cloudy and it started to rain – the views weren't very good. We bought some umbrellas and went to see a concert. When we came out – guess what? It was warm and sunny again!

c

Saturday, March 17

I can't believe it – it's 11:00 p.m. and we're still in Berlin Airport! It's really cold, and it snowed all day. We took a taxi to the airport, and when we arrived, we saw that there were no flights. The next flight is tomorrow morning at 7:00 a.m.

d

Sunday, March 18

Finally, we're back home in Ireland. We had bad luck with the weather, but we had a great trip, and we loved Berlin.

Personal Best Write a paragraph about the weather in your town or city in different seasons.

8 LANGUAGE — *there was/were* ■ nature

8C Then and now

1 Match the words in the box with the parts of the picture 1–6.

| sky | field | forest | mountain | river | tree |

1 _____   4 _____
2 _____   5 _____
3 _____   6 _____

Go to Vocabulary practice: nature, page 127

2 Discuss the questions in pairs.
1 Which country is the picture in exercise 1?
2 What nature can you see out of the window?
3 Do you prefer beaches, mountains, or forests? Why?

3 Read the introduction to a radio show. Answer the questions.
1 How many people live in Shenzhen? _____
2 Where does Liu Jiang live now? _____
3 What's her job? _____
4 When was she last in Shenzhen? _____

Then and Now: Shenzhen, China

In the 1970s, Shenzhen was a small fishing town. Today, it is an enormous city of 12 million people. Liu Jiang, a Chinese-American writer from Chicago, lived in Shenzhen as a child. Listen as she returns to the city for the first time in 30 years.

Sunday, June 28, 9:00 p.m.

Radio 7

4 ▶ 8.8 Listen to the radio show. Check (✓) the things that Shenzhen had 30 years ago and has today.

	Fields	Forest	Tall buildings	River	Train station	Airport	College
Shenzhen 30 years ago							
Shenzhen today							

5 A ▶ 8.8 Match the halves to make sentences and questions. Listen again and check.

1 **There were** fields   a or buses?
2 **There was** a forest   b here before.
3 **There were no** cars   c – everyone had bikes.
4 **Was there** public transportation d to travel around the country?
5 **Were there** any trains   e where we played.
6 **There was no** college   f around the town.

B Look at the words in **bold** in sentences 1–6 again. Choose the correct options to complete the rules. Then read the Grammar box.

1 We use *there was* and *there were* to talk about *the present / the past*.
2 We use *there was* and *there was no* with *singular / plural* nouns.
3 We use *there were* and *there were no* with *singular / plural* nouns.

there was/were ■ nature   LANGUAGE 8C

Grammar *there was/were*

Affirmative:
There was a train station.
There were lots of trees.

Negative:
There was no airport.
There were no cars. /
There weren't any cars.

Questions
Was there a college?
Were there any stores?

Short answers:
Yes, there was.   No, there wasn't.
Yes, there were. No, there weren't.

Go to Grammar practice: *there was/were*, page 103

6 Complete the text with the correct forms of *there was/were*.

This is Pompeii in Italy. In A.D. 79, a volcano destroyed the city. But what was life like for the 20,000 people that lived there before?
¹_____ about 200 cafés in the town. They sold eggs, cheese, bread, and fruit. ²_____ also a market.
Children attended class outside or at home, so ³_____ any school buildings. ⁴_____ some doctors, but ⁵_____ no hospital.
⁶_____ a big amphitheater, where ⁷_____ plays and concerts. And of course, ⁸_____ gladiators!

7 A ▶ 8.10 **Pronunciation: sentence stress** Listen and repeat the questions and short answers. Pay attention to the underlined stressed words.

1 Was there a train station?   Yes, there was.
2 Was there an airport?   No, there wasn't.
3 Were there any trees?   Yes, there were.
4 Were there any cars?   No, there weren't.

B ▶ 8.11   In pairs, ask and answer questions 1–4 about Pompeii. Remember to stress the correct words. Listen, check, and repeat.

1 Were there any cafés?
2 Was there a market?
3 Were there any school buildings?
4 Was there a hospital?

Go to Communication practice: Student A page 140, Student B page 148

8 In pairs, look at the pictures and talk about Oxford Street in London in the past. Use the words in the box and your own ideas.

> buses   road   stores   horses and carriages   tall buildings   bus stops   street lights   taxis

There were no buses in the 19th century.

Oxford Street, 19th century   Oxford Street, now

9 How is your town or city different from the past? In pairs, talk about the differences.

There was a movie theater on Panama Street, but now there's a grocery store.

Personal Best Write about where you lived when you were a child.

8 SKILLS SPEAKING starting and ending a phone call at work ■ buying a ticket

8D A trip to Canada

1 Ask and answer the questions in pairs.

1 Why do you usually travel?
   a for work or study   b to visit friends or family   c to go on vacation   d other
2 How do you prefer to travel? Why?
   a to take the train   b to fly   c to drive   d other
3 How do you usually book your tickets when you travel?
   a online   b on the phone   c at a travel agent's   d other

2 A ▶ 8.12 Watch or listen to the first part of *Learning Curve*. Answer the questions.

1 Why does Marc want to travel?
2 How does he prefer to travel?
3 How does he book the tickets?

B ▶ 8.12 Are the sentences true (T) or false (F)? Watch or listen again, and check.

1 Marc works with technology. _____
2 He never buys tickets online. _____
3 He loves flying. _____
4 Clarisse is Marc's friend. _____
5 It's hot and sunny in California. _____
6 The trip to Montreal takes 11 hours. _____

3 ▶ 8.13 Complete the questions with the words in the box. Listen and check.

| arrive how leave when return |

1 **Clarisse** _____ do you want to leave?
  Marc March 11.
2 **Clarisse** When would you like to _____ ?
  Marc March 21.
3 **Marc** What time does the train _____ ?
  Clarisse The train leaves from New York at 8:15 a.m.
4 **Marc** And when does it _____ in Montreal?
  Clarisse 7:11 p.m.
5 **Marc** So, _____ much is it?
  Clarisse It's $138 for a round-trip ticket.

Conversation builder | buying a ticket

Customer:
I'd like a one-way/round-trip ticket to …
What time does the train/bus/flight leave?
What time/When does it arrive?
How much is it?

Assistant:
What kind of ticket would you like?
Would you like a one-way or round-trip ticket?
When do you want to return/leave?
It's … for a one-way/round-trip ticket.

4 Read the Conversation builder. Then, in pairs, make conversations to buy the tickets.

A *I'd like a one-way ticket to San Diego, please.*   **B** *When would you like to leave?*

Ticket type: ONE-WAY
Adults: ONE
From: LOS ANGELES
To: SAN DIEGO
Date: FEB 8
Time: 9:55 a.m.
Arrival: 12:54 p.m.
Price: $37.00

OUTBOUND
Flight: AA 1503
Departing from: Chicago O'Hare
December 4, 8:25 a.m.
Arriving at: Cancún
December 4, 1:06 p.m.

RETURN
Flight: AA 2348
Departing from: Cancún
December 18, 2:00 p.m.
Arriving at: Chicago O'Hare
December 18, 4:57 p.m.
Price: $382.00

starting and ending a phone call at work ■ buying a ticket **SPEAKING** **SKILLS** **8D**

5 A ▶ 8.14 Watch or listen to the second part of the show. Do you think Marc enjoyed his trip? Why/Why not?

B ▶ 8.14 Choose the correct options to complete the sentences. Watch or listen again, and check.

1 Marc asks Clarisse about ____ .
   a places to eat   b places to stay
   c public transportation
2 The Wi-Fi in Montreal's not good when ____ .
   a it snows   b it rains   c it's windy
3 On his trip, Marc helped people with their ____ .
   a coffee and sandwiches   b French   c Wi-Fi

6 ▶ 8.15 Listen to the phrases from the conversations. Are they for starting or ending a phone call?

1 Hello, *Bon Voyage Travel*. This is Clarisse.
2 Thanks. Goodbye.
3 Hello, my name is Marc Kim. I'm Penny's friend.
4 Thanks for calling.

> **Skill** — starting and ending a phone call at work
>
> When you speak on the telephone, remember to give important information and be polite.
> • When you answer the phone, say *Hello* and identify yourself or your company: *Hello, Learning Curve. Hello, this is Clarisse.*
> • When you call someone, say who you are: *Hello, this is ... , My name's ...*
> • When the conversation finishes, thank the person who called and say goodbye: *Thanks for calling. Thanks for your call.*

7 ▶ 8.16 Complete the conversations with the missing words. Listen and check.

Brad   Hello, *Easy Travel*. Brad ¹_____ .
Jenny Hi, ² _____ is Jenny Foster. I'd like a one-way ticket to Seoul from Sydney, please.
...
Brad   OK, Jenny. You leave on June 15 at 08:15 and you arrive in Seoul at 17:05.
Jenny Thanks very much.
Brad   You're welcome. Thanks for your ³ _____ .
Jenny ⁴ _____ .

Go to Communication practice: Student A page 140, Student B page 148

8 A **PREPARE** Choose a type of transportation and write down the information.

train

bus

plane

ferry

• where you want to go
• what type of ticket you want

• when you want to leave
• if/when you want to return

B **PRACTICE** Sit back-to-back with a partner. Act out a telephone call to buy a ticket. Then switch roles.

C **PERSONAL BEST** Listen to another pair. Write down three things that they do well.

Personal Best   Write a conversation between a customer and a travel agent about a new trip.

7 and 8 — REVIEW and PRACTICE

Grammar

1 Choose the correct options to complete the questions and sentences.

1 Where _____ last night?
 a you were
 b were you
 c you was

2 Our taxi driver _____ very friendly.
 a wasn't
 b not was
 c weren't

3 She _____ work at 7:00 p.m. last night.
 a did finish
 b finishes
 c finished

4 _____ soccer last weekend?
 a Did you play
 b You did play
 c You played

5 They _____ to Oslo for a meeting.
 a did fly
 b flied
 c flew

6 We had a map, so we _____ lost.
 a didn't get
 b didn't got
 c not got

7 _____ a restaurant in your hotel?
 a There was
 b Was there
 c Were there

8 _____ two police officers in the street last night.
 a There was
 b They were
 c There were

2 Rewrite the questions and sentences in the simple past.

1 Does she play tennis with Laura?
 _____ last weekend?

2 There are two eggs in the refrigerator.
 _____ last night.

3 I don't have time for breakfast.
 _____ this morning.

4 I ride my bike to work.
 _____ yesterday.

5 Do you go to the gym?
 _____ last Saturday?

6 He gets on the 8:00 a.m. train.
 _____ yesterday.

3 Complete the text with the simple past form of the verbs in parentheses.

Birds for friends

In many countries, people give food to birds in parks or in their yards. But Gabi Mann from Seattle in the U.S. has a very special relationship with the birds in her neighborhood – they bring *her* gifts!
The story ¹_____ (start) when Gabi ²_____ (be) four years old. She ³_____ (have) some food in the car and when she ⁴_____ (get out), the food fell on the ground. There ⁵_____ (be) a crow near the car and it ⁶_____ (fly) down to eat the food. After that, Gabi ⁷_____ (not eat) all of her lunch at school. Instead, she kept some and ⁸_____ (give) it to the birds on the way home. In 2013, she ⁹_____ (help) more birds and put food and water in the yard every morning. One day, the crows started bringing things like buttons, rocks, small pieces of metal or plastic, and even jewelry for Gabi. ¹⁰_____ they _____ (want) to say "thank you" to her? Gabi thinks so. She collects these "gifts" and she now has more than 100. Her favorite is a metal heart. "It shows me how much they love me," she says.

Vocabulary

1 Put the words in the box in the correct columns.

| summer April cold field fifth fall first flower grass hot March May mountain winter ninth October second spring warm wet |

Months	Ordinal numbers	Weather	Nature	Seasons

76

REVIEW and PRACTICE 7 and 8

2 Circle the word that is different. Explain your answers.

1	artist	musician	winter	dancer
2	week	rain	month	year
3	beach	dry	ocean	river
4	spring	summer	fall	windy
5	snow	ride	sail	fly
6	foggy	sunny	sky	cloudy
7	forest	sixth	third	fourth
8	king	queen	tree	politician

3 Choose the correct options to complete the sentences.

1 The summer in India is very _____ and wet.
   a hot   **b** sun   **c** cold

2 My sister _____ the train at King Street Station.
   a gets on   **b** gets in   **c** gets out

3 Don't _____ your bus! It leaves in five minutes.
   a take   **b** miss   **c** get lost

4 There are lots of big trees in this _____ .
   a flower   **b** foggy   **c** forest

5 Did you _____ your ticket to New York yesterday?
   a fly   **b** book   **c** sail

6 He _____ of the car at the police station.
   a got out   **b** got off   **c** got on

7 The _____ played the piano very well.
   a musician   **b** athlete   **c** dancer

8 It was a beautiful day, so we _____ to the park.
   a walked   **b** watched   **c** worked

9 With my smartphone, I never _____ in a new city.
   a miss   **b** get out   **c** get lost

10 You can't swim in the _____ . It's very dangerous.
   a river   **b** field   **c** sky

4 Complete the sentences with the words in the box.

> ago   6:00   at   summer   in (x2)   Friday
> last   on (x2)   yesterday   July

1 I went to Greece _____ year on vacation.
2 Did you meet your friends on _____ ?
3 He started work _____ 7:00 this morning.
4 We usually go shopping _____ Saturday.
5 We can take the train at _____ .
6 His birthday is _____ June.
7 He started a new job two weeks _____ .
8 _____ fourth is a national holiday.
9 I played tennis with my brother _____ .
10 What did you do _____ the weekend?
11 She lived in Bogotá _____ 2016.
12 We didn't go on vacation in the _____ .

Personal Best

Lesson 7A
Name five celebrities with different jobs.

Lesson 8A
List five irregular verbs and their simple past forms.

Lesson 7A
Write where you were on two different days last week.

Lesson 8B
Describe the weather in your favorite season.

Lesson 7B
Write the birthdays of four friends or family members.

Lesson 8B
Write three sentences with *very, pretty,* and *really,* and an adjective.

Lesson 7C
Write three sentences beginning *Last year …, Two years ago …,* and *Yesterday … .*

Lesson 8C
Name five things from nature you can see out of the window.

Lesson 7C
List five regular verbs and their simple past forms.

Lesson 8C
Write two sentences about your home as a child. Use *There was …* and *There were … .*

Lesson 7D
Describe what you did yesterday with *First, Then,* and *After that.*

Lesson 8D
Write three sentences for buying a train ticket.

77

UNIT 9 Shopping

LANGUAGE present continuous ■ clothes

9A Street style

1 Match the words in the box with the clothes in the picture.

| belt | jeans | jacket | T-shirt | hat |

1 _____ 2 _____ 3 _____ 4 _____ 5 _____

Go to Vocabulary practice: clothes, page 128

2 Discuss the questions in pairs.
  1 What do you usually wear …
    a at home?   b at work/in class?   c on vacation?
  2 Where do you usually buy your clothes? What's your favorite store?
  3 Do you buy used clothing? Why/Why not?

3 Read the text and answer the questions.
  1 Where is Sukanya from?   3 Why does she buy these clothes?
  2 What type of clothes does she wear?   4 Where does she take Mark?

Fashion Diary with Mark Ashcroft

This week, I'm in Thailand with local fashion blogger Sukanya Tanasan. Sukanya only wears used clothing, but she looks amazing!
"There are some great places to buy clothes in Bangkok," she says. "If I need a new dress, a T-shirt, or shoes, I always go to the markets. You can find really cool clothes there, and they're cheap too!"
Today, Sukanya takes me to the Chatuchak market in Bangkok on a shopping trip.

▶ PLAY   ⬇ DOWNLOAD

4 ▶ 9.2 Listen and check (✓) the things Sukanya buys.
T-shirt ☐   dress ☐   shoes ☐   hat ☐   skirt ☐

5 A ▶ 9.2 Complete the sentences with the words in the box. Listen again and check.

| getting buying taking eating leaving doing |

1 We're _____ the train to Chatuchak market.
2 A lot of people are _____ out here.
3 She's _____ the dress!
4 What's this man _____?
5 Sukanya, you're not _____ the rice!
6 We're _____ the market now.

B Look at sentences 1–6 again and answer the questions. Then read the Grammar box.
1 What are the sentences about? *things happening now / regular events*
2 Which three letters are at the end of the main verbs? _____
3 Which verb do we use before the main verb? *be / do*

78

present continuous ■ clothes **LANGUAGE 9A**

Grammar: present continuous

Things that are happening now

Affirmative:
I**'m going** to the market.
We**'re getting off** the bus.

Negative:
She**'s not having** a drink.
They**'re not wearing** glasses.

Questions and short answers:
Are you **working** today?
Yes, I **am**.   No, I**'m not**.

Go to Grammar practice: present continuous, page 104

6 Complete the phone messages with the present continuous form of the verbs in parentheses.

7 A ▶ 9.4 **Pronunciation:** -ing endings Listen and repeat. Pay attention to the /ɪŋ/ sound in **bold**.

com**ing**   go**ing**   do**ing**   runn**ing**   wait**ing**   stay**ing**

B ▶ 9.5 Say the questions and sentences. Then listen, check and repeat.

1 Where are you going?
2 She's running for her bus.
3 I'm not doing any work.
4 Are you staying?
5 He's coming to the café.
6 We're waiting for a taxi.

Go to Communication practice: Student A page 150, Student B page 149

8 In pairs, ask and answer the question *What is/are … doing?* about the people in the pictures.

A *What's David doing?*
B *I think he's having lunch in a restaurant.*

Jorge ● online

Hi, Jorge, what ¹_____ you _____ (do)?
I ²_____ (go) downtown with my sister.   11:35

Cool! I'm there too.   11:36

Do you want to meet for a coffee in 30 mins? The café on Bridge Street?   11:36

11:37

I ³_____ (sit) next to the window. My sister ⁴_____ (not/stay). She needs to buy a new dress. Are you here?   12:05

I ⁵_____ (get) a coffee. Do you want one?   12:10

⁶_____ you _____ (come) ?!   12:19

I'm sorry. My battery died. I ⁷_____ (run) to the café now.   12:25

Too late. We ⁸_____ (wait) for the bus home.   12:26   12:26

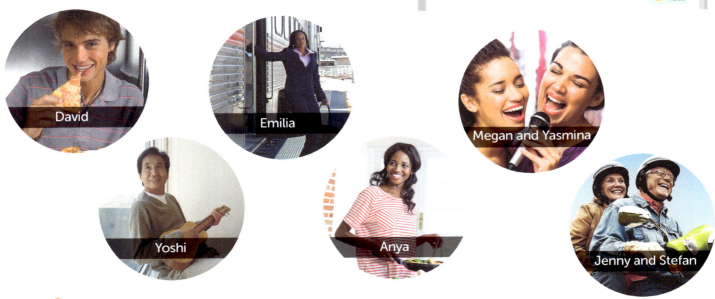

David   Emilia   Megan and Yasmina   Yoshi   Anya   Jenny and Stefan

9 In pairs, describe a classmate. Your partner guesses the person.

A *She's wearing a blue dress, and she's sitting next to Leon.*
B *Is it Malika?*
A *Yes, it is!*

Personal Best   Think of six people you know. Write sentences about what they're doing at the moment.

79

9 SKILLS LISTENING identifying key points ■ filler words ■ feelings

9B How do you feel?

1 Match the words in the box with pictures a–f.

> angry   calm   excited   hungry   thirsty   tired

a  b  c  d  e  f

Go to Vocabulary practice: feelings, page 129

2 ▶9.7 Complete the text with four feelings from exercise 1. Listen and check.

Colors and feelings

Colors can sometimes change how we feel. For example, orange can make us feel happy and ^{1}_____ . A lot of restaurants, for example McDonald's and KFC, use red because it can make us feel ^{2}_____ . Offices often use blue because it makes us ^{3}_____ . But gray's not a popular color for offices because it can make us feel sad or ^{4}_____ .

3 A Look at the picture of Ethan. How does his shirt make you feel?

B ▶9.8 Match the colors in the box with sentences 1–4. Watch or listen to the first part of *Learning Curve* and check.

> orange   blue   white   black   yellow

1 Doctors often wear this color.   _____
2 Firefighters usually wear these colors.   _____ or _____
3 The police in the U.S. wear this color.   _____
4 People wear this color when they're sad. _____

Skill identifying key points

When people speak, try to listen for the important things they say.
- We often emphasize or repeat the most important ideas.
- We sometimes give examples or more information.

4 ▶9.8 Read the Skill box. Then watch or listen again. Check (✓) the **two** key points Ethan talks about.

a Colors can change how we feel. ☐
b Colors are important in festivals all around the world. ☐
c Orange is a popular color for clothes. ☐
d Workers sometimes wear uniforms of the same color. ☐

5 Discuss the questions in pairs.

1 Do you wear a uniform for work?
2 Did you wear a uniform at school?
3 What colors are/were the uniforms?
4 How do/did they make you feel?

identifying key points ■ filler words ■ feelings   **LISTENING**   SKILLS   **9B**

6 ▶ 9.9 Watch or listen to the rest of the show. Match the feelings in the box with the people.

bored   excited   scared   hungry   thirsty

 Udo
 Akiko
 Penny
 Bob

1 _____   2 _____   3 _____   4 _____ and _____

7 ▶ 9.9 Watch or listen again. Choose the correct options to complete the key points.
1 Udo _____ .
  a makes his own clothes   b buys expensive clothes   c only wears bright colors
2 Akiko _____ .
  a doesn't like *Learning Curve*   b doesn't like Ethan's shirt   c is late for class
3 Bob _____ .
  a loves the color yellow   b wears a uniform for work   c wants to eat something

8 Ask and answer the questions in the boxes.

What are you wearing today?   What colors are the clothes?   How do they make you feel?

9 ▶ 9.10 Read the two extracts. Can you understand them without the missing words? Listen and write the missing words.

1 _____ Penny, what are people wearing today? Do you see a lot of colors on the streets of New York?

2 _____ , people are leaving work at the moment. Let's see what they're wearing.

Listening builder   filler words

When people speak, they often say short words while they are thinking of what to say. You can ignore these words – they don't really mean anything.
So, what are you, *uh*, wearing today?
Well, I'm wearing blue jeans and, *um*, this red T-shirt.

10 ▶ 9.11 Read the Listening builder. Then listen to the description of the photo. Check (✔) the sentences the speaker says.
1 a This photo is of a young girl in a school. ☐
  b In this photo, there's a young girl at school. ☐
  c The photo shows a young girl in school. ☐
2 a And she's wearing a gray uniform and glasses. ☐
  b And she has a long gray uniform and glasses. ☐
  c And she's wearing a uniform and some glasses. ☐
3 a She's standing near the teacher's desk. ☐
  b In the class, there are no teachers. ☐
  c I think she's waiting for the teacher. ☐

11 Discuss the questions in pairs.
1 What are your favorite colors?
2 How do they make you feel?
3 Which do you not like?
4 How do they make you feel?

Personal Best   Describe the colors in the rooms in your house or apartment and say how they make you feel.

81

9 LANGUAGE — *how often* + expressions of frequency ■ shopping

9C Love it or hate it?

1 Complete phrases 1–5 with the words in the box.

> buy pay shop sell try on

1 _____ shoes
2 _____ by credit card
3 _____ fruit
4 _____ online
5 _____ a car

Personal Best

Go to Vocabulary practice: shopping, page 130

2 Do the questionnaire in pairs. Write down your partner's answers. Then go to page 147 and look at the results.

Shopping – do you love it or hate it?

1 How often do you go to a shopping mall?
a Never! I hate malls.
b I only go when I need some new clothes.
c I go there every week. I love it!

2 Do you spend a lot of money on clothes and shoes?
a No, I don't. I usually buy used clothes.
b When I have a special occasion – once or twice a year.
c Yes, I do. Clothes are very important to me.

3 How often do you shop online?
a Not often. Maybe once a year.
b A few times a month.
c Very often. Three or four times a week.

4 How do you feel if you need to buy a present for someone?
a Bored. I prefer to give cash as a present.
b Happy. I can find something in a local store.
c Really excited! I can go shopping all day on Saturday!

5 How do you usually pay when you go shopping?
a I pay with cash. I never spend money that I don't have.
b I sometimes pay with cash and sometimes by card.
c I usually pay by credit card.

3 A Complete the questions and sentences from the questionnaire with the words in the box.

> how every times twice often once

1 How _____ do you go to a shopping mall?
2 I go there _____ week.
3 Once or _____ a year.
4 _____ often do you shop online?
5 Maybe _____ a year.
6 Three or four _____ a week.

B Which tense do we use to talk about the frequency of events? *simple present* / *present continuous*
Read the Grammar box.

how often + expressions of frequency ▪ shopping   LANGUAGE **9C**

Grammar: how often + expressions of frequency

How often do you go shopping?

| I go shopping | once a
twice a
three/four times a
every | day/week/month/year |

Go to Grammar practice: *how often + expressions of frequency*, page 104

4 A ▶9.14 **Pronunciation:** sentence stress Listen and repeat the expressions of frequency. Pay attention to the underlined stressed words.

1 <u>once</u> a <u>day</u>
2 <u>twice</u> a <u>year</u>
3 <u>three</u> <u>times</u> a <u>month</u>
4 <u>every</u> <u>day</u> and <u>every</u> <u>night</u>

B ▶9.15 Say the sentences. Pay attention to the sentence stress. Listen, check and repeat.

1 I call my girlfriend twice a day.
2 We go to the movies every month.
3 They shop online three times a week.
4 My grandparents visit every year.

Go to Communication practice: Student A page 141, Student B page 149

5 A Write the questions.

1 How often / you buy someone a present?
   _____
   _____
   _____

4 How often / it snow in your town?
   _____
   _____
   _____

2 How often / your teacher give homework?
   _____
   _____
   _____

5 How often / you go to bed after midnight?
   _____
   _____
   _____

3 How often / you wash your hair?
   _____
   _____
   _____

6 How often / you pay by credit card?
   _____
   _____
   _____

B In pairs, ask and answer the questions.

A *How often do you buy someone a present?*
B *I buy someone a present once or twice a month. How about you?*

6 A Write three true sentences and three false sentences about you with expressions of frequency.
B Read your sentences to your partner. Guess if they are true or false.

A *I go to Singapore twice a year.*
B *I think that's false.*
A *No, it's true! My sister lives there.*

Personal Best Write some more questions about shopping for a questionnaire.

9 SKILLS WRITING describing a photo ▪ describing position

9D Garage sale

1 A What do you do with things you don't use any more?

a Throw them away.   b Take them to a thrift store.   c Sell them online.   d Have a garage sale.

B Discuss the questions in pairs.
1 How often do you buy used things?
2 What type of used things do you buy?
3 Do people have garage sales in your country?
4 Do you think they're a good idea? Why/Why not?

2 A Read the e-mail quickly. What relationship is the writer to Patrick?

B Read the e-mail again. Match the names in the box with the people in the picture.

Bill Sandra Evie Eddie

Hi Patrick,

How are you?

a We had a garage sale yesterday. It was at our house, and we sold some old clothes, books and other things.

b Here's a photo. The man on the right is our friend, Bill. He's looking at our old things. His wife Sandra is on the left, and the girl in the middle is their daughter, Evie. She's trying on my old hat. There's an old skateboard at the bottom of the photo – I think it's your dad's. The man at the top of the picture is our neighbor, Eddie. He's looking at a pair of Grandpa's old pants!

c We made about $100! We bought some new chairs for the yard with the money.

E-mail me soon with your news.

Grandma

3 A Match paragraphs a–c with the parts of the e-mail 1–3.
1 description of photo ____   2 what happened after ____   3 introduction ____

B What tenses are the verbs in paragraphs a–c? Read the Skill box.

Skill describing a photo

When we describe a photo, we:
- explain who the people are: *The man on the right is our friend, Bill.*
- use the present continuous to say what they are doing: *She's trying on my old hat.*
- use *there is/are* to say what things are in the picture: *There's an old skateboard ...*

describing a photo ■ **describing position** **WRITING** **SKILLS 9D**

4 Complete Patrick's reply with the correct form of the verbs in parentheses.

Dear Grandma,

I'm very well, thanks. That's great about the garage sale!

I ¹_____ (go) to Bristol last Saturday with some friends. We ²_____ (take) the train in the morning, and we ³_____ (explore) the city.

Here's a photo. The girl on the left is Sara, and the girl in the middle is Lisa. They ⁴_____ (be) my classmates from college. They ⁵_____ (try) to find the Clifton Suspension Bridge on the map. Lisa's boyfriend, Shaun, is on the right. He ⁶_____ (take) a photo of some street art.

It was a fun day out, but we ⁷_____ (be) all really tired when we ⁸_____ (get) home!

Love Patrick x

5 Match the halves to make sentences. Check your answers in the e-mails.

1 The man on
2 The girl in
3 There's an old skateboard at
4 The man at
5 The girl on

a the left is Sara.
b the middle is their daughter, Evie.
c the right is our friend, Bill.
d the top of the picture is our neighbor, Eddie.
e the bottom of the photo.

Text builder describing position

▶ on the right   ▲ at the top   ✕ in the middle
◀ on the left   ▼ at the bottom ◣ in the corner

6 A Read the Text builder. Then write sentences.

1 that / my brother / right   _That's my brother on the right._
2 my friend Casey / middle   _____
3 there / a cat / corner   _____
4 that / my cousin / top   _____
5 there / more people / left   _____

B In pairs, take a photo of some of your classmates. Describe the photo using phrases from the Text builder.

That's Nacho on the left, and Lola is on the right. There's a blue purse in the corner. It's Lola's purse.

7 A PREPARE Choose one of the photos. Imagine that you took it. Make notes to answer the questions.

1 When and where did you take the photo?
2 Who are the people in the photo?
3 What are they doing?
4 What happened after you took the photo?

B PRACTICE Write an e-mail. Introduce the photo, describe it, and say what happened after you took it.

C PERSONAL BEST Exchange e-mails with your partner and read his/her work. Check the tenses of the verbs and prepositions for describing position. Can you improve anything?

Personal Best   Write an e-mail describing one of your own photos.

UNIT 10 Time out

LANGUAGE present continuous for future plans ■ free-time activities

10A What are you doing on the weekend?

1 A Look at the poster for a music festival. Discuss the questions in pairs.

1. Do you know this music festival?
2. Where and when is the festival?
3. Do you like music festivals? Why/Why not?
4. What can you see in the pictures?

B Complete the text with the words in the box.

visit   go   watch   have   stay

COACHELLA Music and Arts Festival

Win tickets for an incredible Coachella experience

 Call 08081 570000 and tell us why you want to go.

1 _____ to all the concerts
2 _____ in a luxury tent
3 _____ the art area and see amazing sculptures
4 _____ movies at night
5 _____ a good time!

April 14–16
Coachella Valley, California

Go to Vocabulary practice: free-time activities, page 131

2 ▶ 10.2 Read and listen to the conversation between two friends. Where is Alex going this weekend?

Alex Guess what I'm doing this weekend.
Dan I don't know. Are you visiting your family again?
Alex No, I'm not. I'm going to a music festival – Coachella! I won tickets in a contest.
Dan Coachella? No way! Which bands are playing?
Alex Radiohead is playing on Friday, and Lady Gaga on Saturday.
Dan That's awesome. Are you going on your own?
Alex No, the prize was two tickets.
Dan Two tickets? You know, I'm not doing anything this weekend …
Alex I'm sorry, Dan. I'm going with my mom.
Dan Your mom?
Alex Yeah, she loves Lady Gaga. We're driving there tonight and then we're staying in a tent all weekend!
Dan Well, have a good time. Tell me all about it on Monday, OK?

3 Are the sentences true (T) or false (F)? Check your answers in the conversation.

1 Dan's going to Coachella with Alex. ____
2 Lady Gaga's playing on Saturday. ____
3 They're driving to the festival tonight. ____
4 They're staying in a hotel all weekend. ____

86

present continuous for future plans ■ free-time activities   **LANGUAGE** **10A**

4 A Look at the sentences in exercise 3 again. Answer the questions.
   1 Which tense are the verbs? *simple present / simple past / present continuous*
   2 When do the actions happen? *in the past / now / in the future*

B Find more examples of this tense in the conversation in exercise 2. Then read the Grammar box.

| **Grammar** | **present continuous for future plans** |

Affirmative:
I'm going to a music festival this weekend.
We're visiting a museum tomorrow.

Negative:
She's not going to the concert tonight.
They're not staying in a hotel.

Questions and short answers:
Are you having a party in the summer?
Yes, I am. No, I'm not.

Go to Grammar practice: present continuous for future plans, page 105

5 A ▶10.5 **Pronunciation: sentence stress** Listen and repeat the questions and answers from the conversation in exercise 2. Pay attention to the underlined stressed words.
   1 Are you visiting your family?   No, I'm not.
   2 Which bands are playing?   Radiohead is playing on Friday.

B ▶10.6 Match the questions with answers a–c. Ask and answer the questions in pairs with the correct stress. Listen, check and repeat.
   1 What are you doing this weekend?   a I'm taking the bus.
   2 How are you getting there?   b Yes, I am.
   3 Are you staying with friends?   c I'm going to the beach.

6 Look at Rosie's diary on her smartphone. In pairs, ask and answer the question *What's she doing ...?* with the times in the box.

> ~~this morning~~   on Friday   tomorrow   on the weekend
> the day after tomorrow   this evening

A *What's she doing this morning?*
B *She's having coffee with Kate.*

Go to Communication practice:
Student A page 141, Student B page 149

7 A ▶10.7 Use the words to write questions in the present continuous. Listen to the conversation and check.
   1 What / you / do / on the weekend?
   _____
   2 Who / you / go / with?
   _____
   3 How / you / get / there?
   _____
   4 When / you / leave?
   _____
   5 Where / you / stay?
   _____

B ▶10.7 Listen again and write Cheryl's answers to the questions.

8 A Make notes about your plans for the weekend. They can be real or imaginary.
   B In pairs, ask and answer the questions in exercise 7 about your plans.
   A *What are you doing on the weekend?*   **B** *I'm having a barbecue with my friends.*

Personal Best   Write a paragraph about your "perfect" weekend.

10 SKILLS | **READING** scanning for information ■ the imperative ■ types of music and movies

10B What's on?

1 ▶10.8 Listen and match the words in the box with the types of music and movies.

> classical   science fiction   action   jazz   electronic   romance

1 _____ 2 _____ 3 _____ 4 _____ 5 _____ 6 _____

Go to Vocabulary practice: types of music and movies, page 132

2 Look at the webpage on page 89. What type of website is it? Do you use websites like this?

> **Skill   scanning for information**
>
> **"Scanning" means looking quickly at a text to find specific information.**
> • Underline the key word(s) in the question.
> • Look for the word(s) in the text quickly. Use your finger to help you.
> • When you find the word, read the information to answer the question.

3 A Read the Skill box. Then read questions 1–4 and scan the text for the answers.
The key words are underlined.

1 What time does the concert start? _____
2 Where is the art exhibition? _____
3 How much is a movie ticket for children? _____
4 Which event is free to enter? _____

B Read questions 1–4 and underline the key words. Then scan the text for the answers.

1 What's the name of the movie theater in the city? _____
2 How old do you need to be to try speed dating? _____
3 Which event costs less if you buy tickets online? _____
4 Who's playing electronic music tonight? _____

4 Look at the text and discuss the questions in pairs.

1 Which events do you want to go to? Why?   2 Which events are you not interested in? Why?

5 Complete the sentences from the text with the correct words.

1 Don't _____ it!   3 _____ all night.
2 _____ to our Speed Dating night!   4 _____ very scared!

> **Text builder   the imperative**
>
> **We use the imperative to give instructions.**
> *Book early!   Open the window!   Don't be late!   Don't forget about the party!*

6 Read the Text builder. Then complete the sentences with the affirmative or negative imperative of the verbs in the box.

> call   listen   talk   sit   open   be

1 _____ down, please. I can't see the movie.   4 _____ the window, please. It's very hot.
2 The concert starts at 7:45, so _____ late.   5 Please _____ in the library. I'm trying to read.
3 _____ to this great song. I love it!   6 _____ me today because I'm working.

7 Discuss the questions in pairs.

1 What's your favorite type of music?   4 What type of movies do you like?
2 When do you listen to music?   5 What was the last movie you saw?
3 How often do you go to concerts/clubs?   6 How often do you go to the movies?

88

scanning for information • the imperative • types of music and movies   READING   SKILLS   10B

What's On

Events in your area: **Saturday, June 9**   Sort by: Date

Visitors
Science-fiction adventure. When aliens arrive on Earth, do they want to help people – or start a war?
ABC Movie Theater, 6:30 p.m. 9:00 p.m. 11:30 p.m.
Tickets $10. Under 16: $8

 Buy Tickets

Anderson .Paak in concert
Anderson .Paak brings his mix of jazz, hip-hop, and rock to the city. Don't miss it!
Royal Arena, 8:00 p.m.
Tickets $17.50

 Sold Out

Romeo and Juliet
William Shakespeare's great love story. A boy and a girl find love on the streets of Verona.
King's Theater, 7:15 p.m.
Tickets $18.00

 Sold Out

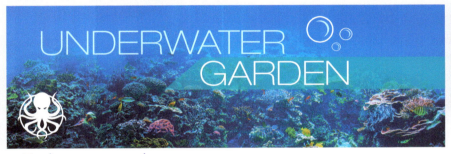

Underwater garden
Dance all night as DJ Octopus plays the latest in electronic music from around the world.
Club Infinity, 10:00 p.m.–late   **Admission** $8.00 (Over 18 only)

Buy Tickets

Hot Potato
Enjoy an evening of comedy with Sally Quentin. "Really funny" *The Daily Times*. Book online and save $5.
Comedy Club, 7:00 p.m.
Tickets $15 at the door

Buy Tickets

Looking for love?
Are you single? Do you want to find that special person? Come to our Speed Dating night – the fun way to meet new people!
Union Coffee Shop, 6:30 p.m.
Admission $15. Minimum age 21

 Buy Tickets

Book reading with Joe Arnott
Joe Arnott reads from his new horror story, *Play With Fire*. Be scared, be very scared!
Forest Hill Library, 8:00 p.m.
Admission free. Over 16 only

 Reserve

Picasso's portraits
Exhibition of paintings and sculptures by one of the most popular artists of the twentieth century.
Trinidad Gallery
Tickets $12.50

Buy Tickets

Personal Best Write information about three events in your town or city. Use imperatives.

10 LANGUAGE   question review ■ sports and games

10C Royal hobbies

1 Complete the sports and games with the verbs *go*, *play* and *do*.

1 _____ tennis   2 _____ karate   3 _____ running   4 _____ rock climbing   5 _____ video games   6 _____ yoga

Go to Vocabulary practice: sports and games, page 133

2 In pairs, ask and answer the question *Do you …?* with the correct verbs and the sports and games in the box.

A *Do you go bike riding?*   B *Yes, I do. I usually go bike riding once a week.*

| bike riding   swimming   soccer   pilates   gymnastics   basketball   chess   karate   skiing |

3 A Who are the people in the picture? Read the text and check. What do you know about them?

B ▶ 10.11 Guess which three activities in exercise 1 the people do. Listen to the interview and check.

4 A ▶ 10.11 Complete the interviewer's questions with the words in the box. Listen again and check.

| was   where   how   does   is   what |

1 _____ does he relax?
2 _____ is his favorite game?
3 _____ did she go to college?
4 _____ she good at sports?
5 _____ William exercise a lot too?
6 _____ he training for a marathon now?

B Look at questions 1–6 again.

1 Which questions do you answer with *yes* or *no*? ___ ___ ___
2 Which questions do you answer with specific information? ___ ___ ___

7:00 pm
Relaxing with the Royals

What do Prince Harry, Prince William and his wife Kate, the Duchess of Cambridge, do in their free time? Royal expert Jenny Brown joins us to talk about how the young royals relax.

5 A Match the tenses in the box with the questions in 4A.

| simple past   present continuous   simple present (x2)   simple present of *be*   simple past of *be* |

1 _____ 2 _____ 3 _____ 4 _____ 5 _____ 6 _____

B Match the words in the box with the parts of the question 1–4. Then read the Grammar box.

| subject   question word   main verb   auxiliary verb |

1 What _____   2 do _____   3 they _____   4 do _____ in their free time?

question review ■ sports and games   LANGUAGE 10C

Grammar | question review

Most verbs: (question word) + auxiliary verb + subject + main verb:
Where do you live? *What are you doing?* *When did they arrive?*
Does Carla play tennis? *Is he watching TV?* *Did you go running yesterday?*

The verb *be*: (question word) + *be* + subject:
How old are you? *Where was Antonio yesterday?*
Is the milk in the refrigerator? *Were you worried about the exam?*

Go to Grammar practice: question review, page 105

6 A ▶ 10.14 **Pronunciation:** Intonation in questions Listen and repeat the questions. Pay attention to the intonation that goes up (↗) or down (↘).

questions with question words
1 Which movies do you like? ↘
2 Where are they going? ↘

yes/no questions
3 Is she from Japan? ↗
4 Did you stay in a hotel? ↗

B ▶ 10.15 Say the questions with the correct intonation. Listen, check and repeat. Then ask and answer the questions in pairs.

1 What are you doing tonight?
2 Did you cook dinner yesterday?
3 Where were you at 7:00 this morning?
4 How often do you take the bus?
5 Is it raining right now?
6 Does our teacher like pop music?

Go to Communication practice: Student A page 141, Student B page 150

7 A ▶ 10.16 Order the words to make questions 1–6. Listen and check.
B ▶ 10.16 In pairs, ask and answer the questions. Listen again and check.

Estonian fashion model Carmen Kass plays chess.

1 start / did / when / she
_____ ?
2 she / how / did / learn
_____ ?

American singer Elvis Presley did karate.

3 karate / at / was / good / he
_____ ?
4 where / do / did / it / he
_____ ?

American actor Lucy Liu goes rock climbing.

5 go / how / rock climbing / she / does / often
_____ ?
6 dangerous / is / it
_____ ?

8 Choose a sport or game that you play. In pairs, ask and answer the questions in the boxes.

- What sport or game do you play?
- When did you start?
- Where do you play it?
- How often do you play it?
- Are you playing it this weekend?
- Is it difficult?
- Is it expensive?
- How did you learn?
- Who do you play it with?
- What do you need to play it?

Personal Best Write a paragraph about a sport or game you enjoy.

10 SKILLS SPEAKING showing interest ■ asking about a tourist attraction

10D Where are we going now?

1 Look at the pictures and answer the questions.

1 Which tourist attractions can you see?
2 Which countries are they in?
3 Do you want to visit them? Why/Why not?
4 What tourist attractions are there in your town/city?

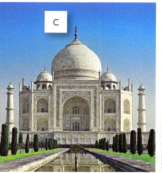

2 A ▶ 10.17 Watch or listen to the first part of *Learning Curve*. Where is Ethan? Who does he meet?

B ▶ 10.17 Choose the correct options to complete the sentences. Watch or listen again and check.

1 Flushing Meadows is famous for its *soccer stadium / tennis stadium*.
2 There were two World's Fairs in the park – in 1939 and in *1964 / 1974*.
3 There is a *science museum / design museum* in the park.
4 Ethan, Penny, and Taylor are meeting Marc in *half an hour / an hour*.
5 Marc and Taylor *know / don't know* each other.

3 ▶ 10.18 Listen and complete the questions in the conversation.

Taylor So what time ¹_____ the Hall of Science _____ ?
Ethan It opens at 10:00 am.
Penny What ²_____ _____ to do if it rains?
Ethan Well, we can stay inside and look at exhibits all day.
Penny OK. Sounds good. When ³_____ it _____ ?
Ethan 6:00 pm.
Taylor OK, great. So, what ⁴_____ we _____ now?
Ethan We're meeting our friend Marc from *Learning Curve*, at the Information Desk.

Conversation builder   asking about a tourist attraction

What time does it open/close? *Is there a café/restaurant/gift shop?*
Which days is it open?   *What is there to do if it rains?*
How do you get there?   *Are there any special events?*

4 A Read the Conversation builder. Then look at the information about a tourist attraction on page 93. Ask and answer questions in pairs.

A *What time does it open?*   **B** *It opens at 9:30 a.m.*

B Do you want to visit this attraction? Why/Why not?

showing interest ■ asking about a tourist attraction SPEAKING SKILLS 10D

Fun days out Legoland > Plan your trip   Week: September 13–19

Monday	Tuesday	Wednesday	Thursday	Friday	Saturday	Sunday

● 9:30 a.m. – 5:00 p.m. ($30)   ● 9:30 a.m. – 6:00 p.m. ($35)   ● Closed

Weather: Most attractions are outside. Umbrellas are available from the gift shop. Inside attractions include: Wells Fargo Fun Town 4D Theater, Imagination Zone and Pirates' Cove.

Food & drink: Fun Town Pizza & Pasta, Castle Burger and many more.

Getting there:
By car: Legoland is on International Drive (parking available).
By bus: Take the shuttle bus from the Orlando Eye.

December 31: Kids' New Year's Eve fireworks show

5 A ▶ 10.19 Watch or listen to the second part of the show. How many exhibits do Penny, Marc, Ethan, and Taylor see in the Hall of Science?

B ▶ 10.19 Are the sentences true (T) or false (F)? Watch or listen again and check.

1 Tickets for the Hall of Science cost $15. ____
2 There are almost 450 exhibits. ____
3 Marc and Ethan buy tickets for a 3D movie. ____
4 Taylor doesn't like flying. ____
5 Taylor wants a flying car. ____
6 They decide to eat pizza. ____

Penny   Ethan   Marc   Taylor

6 ▶ 10.20 Match the sentences with the responses. Listen, check and repeat the responses.

1 It costs $15, but we paid for you.
2 What about *Journey into Space*? It's a 3D movie.
3 We're hungry, and we're eating a very large pizza.

a OK. Sounds good.
b Oh really? Thanks!
c That sounds interesting!

Skill showing interest

When people speak to you, it's important to show that you're listening.
• Use expressions: *Oh really? That sounds good. Great.*
• Use intonation to sound interested.

7 A ▶ 10.21 Read the Skill box. Then listen to conversations 1–4. Which response sounds more interested: *a* or *b*?

1 I'm visiting my family this weekend. ____
2 My sister goes rock climbing every week. ____
3 There's a new comedy at the movie theater. ____
4 We went to the beach yesterday. ____

B ▶ 10.22 Listen and repeat the interested responses.

Go to Communication practice: Students A and B, page 150

8 A PREPARE In pairs, invent a tourist attraction and write information about it. Include:

• the days and times it is open
• the price of tickets
• what you can do
• how to get there
• stores and restaurants
• special events

B PRACTICE Exchange your information with another pair. Then ask and answer questions about the tourist attraction. Remember to show you're interested.

A *What time does the museum open?*   B *It opens at 9:30 a.m.*   A *OK, great.*

C PERSONAL BEST Listen to the other pair. Do they ask questions well? Do they show interest?

Personal Best Write about a tourist attraction in your town/city.

9 and 10 REVIEW and PRACTICE

Grammar

1 Check (✓) the correct sentences.

1 a I can't talk now. I'm doing my homework.
   b I can't talk now. I do my homework.
   c I can't talk now. I did my homework.
2 a They not working right now.
   b They're not working right now.
   c They don't working right now.
3 a What often do you go to the gym?
   b How often do you go to the gym?
   c How much often do you go to the gym?
4 a I see my brother three times at year.
   b I see my brother three times for year.
   c I see my brother three times a year.
5 a What are you doing tomorrow?
   b What do you do tomorrow?
   c What you are doing tomorrow?
6 a He not is coming to the party tonight.
   b He's not coming to the party tonight.
   c He doesn't come to the party tonight.
7 a What time did the train leave?
   b What time the train did leave?
   c What time left the train?
8 a They were at work yesterday?
   b Did they be at work yesterday?
   c Were they at work yesterday?

2 Complete the questions and sentences with the correct form of the verbs in the box.

| cost finish spend go take meet |
| not be not study can buy wear |

1 How often _____ you _____ a shower?
2 Carlos _____ some new boots today. Look – they're really nice.
3 What time _____ you _____ work last night?
4 We _____ shopping in New York next Tuesday.
5 How much _____ your new coat _____ ? Was it expensive?
6 She's in the library, but she _____ . She's texting a friend.
7 _____ you _____ your friends next weekend?
8 He _____ at work yesterday. I think he was sick.
9 Where _____ I _____ some good shoes?
10 How much money _____ you _____ on clothes every month?

3 Complete the text with the correct form of the verbs in parentheses.

The Kinderkook Café

The Kinderkook Café in Amsterdam is a café with a difference – the chefs and waiters are all children! Parents take their children to the café in the afternoon and the children cook a meal. Then, in the evening, the parents return to eat it. Matt Baker talked to one of the parents, Sonja Kroes.

Matt When ¹_____ the café _____ (start)?
Sonja It started in 1981. It's very popular.
Matt What ²_____ the children _____ (cook)?
Sonja They cook pasta, curry, pizza, and lots more. The food is healthy and delicious.
Matt How often ³_____ you _____ (come) here with your daughter?
Sonja We come once a month. Lotte loves it!
Matt ⁴_____ she _____ (work) here today?
Sonja Yes, she is. She ⁵_____ (bake) a cake. Look, she's over there. She ⁶_____ (wear) a pink sweater. And her friend, Stijn, is helping her. They ⁷_____ (have) a good time!
Matt ⁸_____ you _____ (eat) here tonight?
Sonja Yes, I am. I ⁹_____ (come) with my husband and my parents. It was Lotte's birthday yesterday, and she wanted to have a small party here with the family.
Matt That's nice. How old ¹⁰_____ (be) she?
Sonja She's seven.

Vocabulary

1 Put the words in the box in the correct columns.

| volleyball a museum videogames a suit yoga |
| an art gallery shopping bike riding gymnastics |
| karate pants walking tennis my family a belt |

go	do	visit	wear	play

94

REVIEW and PRACTICE 9 and 10

2 Circle the word that is different. Explain your answers.
1. angry   happy   hockey   thirsty
2. skirt   beach   jacket   dress
3. festival   concert   suit   party
4. tent   pay   spend   buy
5. pop   rock   jazz   coat
6. socks   boots   shoes   pants
7. museum   art gallery   sweater   department store
8. money   comedy   romance   drama

3 Choose the correct options to complete the sentences.
1. Can I try _____ this shirt, please?
   a in   b off   c on
2. That store _____ really nice T-shirts.
   a sells   b spends   c pays
3. Let's have dinner _____ home tonight.
   a in   b at   c on
4. Do you want to _____ a movie?
   a go   b look   c watch
5. I don't have any money. Can I pay _____ card?
   a with   b by   c for
6. I usually shop _____ . I don't have time to go to the grocery store.
   a online   b by card   c by cash
7. We're _____ a barbecue this weekend. Would you like to come?
   a having   b staying   c spending
8. We don't accept credit cards here. Can you pay with _____ , please?
   a chess   b cash   c calm

4 Complete the conversation with the words in the box.

| hungry | excited | time | scared |
| horror | bored | happy | tired |

Bella What did you do last night, Ruby?
Ruby Tim and I went to the movie theater. We watched that new ¹_____ movie, *Black Night*.
Bella Were you ²_____ ?
Ruby No, we were ³_____ . It wasn't very good.
Bella That's too bad. Did you do anything after the movie?
Ruby We were really ⁴_____ , so we went to a restaurant.
Bella How was the food?
Ruby It was excellent, so we were ⁵_____ ! What about you? What did you do?
Bella We went to a concert – the Foo Fighters. They're Nick's favorite band. He was very ⁶_____ when he got tickets.
Ruby Did you have a good ⁷_____ ?
Bella Yes, it was great. The concert finished at 1:00 in the morning, so I'm really ⁸_____ today!

95

GRAMMAR PRACTICE

Hello The verb *be* (*I, you*)

We use the verb *be* to give information about people.
I'm Carlos and I'm a teacher.

We usually use contractions in affirmative and negative forms.

You're a student. = You are a student.   *I'm not in Class 3.* = I am not in Class 3.
We form negatives with *not* or the contraction *n't*.

▶ 1.4	I	you
+	I**'m** a student.	You**'re** a teacher.
−	I**'m not** a teacher.	You**'re not** a student.
?	**Am** I in Class 2?	**Are** you in my class?
Y/N	Yes, I **am**. / No, I**'m not**.	Yes, you **are**. / No, you**'re not**.

1 Choose the correct words to complete the sentences and questions.

1 I *'m* / *'re* Harry.
2 You *'m* / *'re* Lola.
3 *Am* / *Are* you a student?
4 *Am I* / *I'm* in Room 3.
5 *Are you* / *You are* late?
6 No, I *'m not* / *aren't*.
7 *Am* / *Are* I in this class?
8 Yes, you *am* / *are*.

◀ Go back to page 4

1A The verb *be* (*he, she, it*)

We use *he*, *she*, and *it* to talk about a person or a thing.
The teacher is Mexican. He's from Puebla.   *My car's not from Germany. It's from Japan.*

We usually use contractions in affirmative and negative forms. We form negatives with *not* or the contraction *n't*.

Akemi's not / Akemi isn't Chinese. = Akemi is not Chinese.
She's Japanese. = She is Japanese.

▶ 1.14	he	she	it
+	Leo**'s** from Peru.	Lucía**'s** Colombian.	The book**'s** Chinese.
−	He**'s not** / He **isn't** from Chile.	She**'s not** / She **isn't** Argentinian.	It**'s not** / It **isn't** Italian.
?	**Is** Ravi from India?	**Is** Ayla Turkish?	**Is** the car German?
Y/N	Yes, he **is**. / No, he**'s not** / he **isn't**.	Yes, she **is**. / No, she**'s not** / she **isn't**.	Yes, it **is**. / No, it**'s not** / it **isn't**.

1 Complete the sentences with the correct words.

1 This is my friend Daniel. He _____ from Spain.
2 Anna's not in class today. _____'s at home.
3 Sophie _____ a student. She's the teacher.
4 This is my car. _____'s a Toyota.
5 **A** Where _____ Ryan Gosling from?
   B He _____ from Canada.
6 **A** What's the capital of Australia? Is _____ Sydney?
   B No, it _____ . It's Canberra.
7 **A** _____ María from Colombia?
   B No, she _____ . She's from Mexico.
8 **A** Is sushi from Japan?
   B Yes, _____ is.

◀ Go back to page 7

1C The verb *be* (*we, you, they*)

We use *we*, *you*, and *they* to talk about people and things in the plural.
The engineers are here. They're from India.   *Susan and I are not happy. We're sad.*

We usually use contractions in affirmative and negative forms. We form negatives with *not* or the contraction *n't*.

You're in Class 3. = You are in Class 3.
The pizzas aren't expensive. = The pizzas are not expensive.

▶ 1.29	we	you	they
+	We**'re** 25 years old.	You**'re** doctors.	They**'re** French.
−	We**'re not** old.	You**'re not** chefs.	Ana and Bea **are not** / **aren't** here.
?	**Are** we sad?	**Are** you happy?	**Are** they in Class 4?
Y/N	Yes, we **are**. / No, we**'re not**.	Yes, you **are**. / No, you**'re not**.	Yes, they **are**. / No, they**'re not**.

1 Rewrite the sentences. Change the words in **bold** to *we*, *you* or *they*.

1 **Elsa and Lucy** are police officers.
   _____
2 **Maite and I** are 21 years old.
   _____
3 Are **you and Wei** from China?
   _____
4 **The doctors** are not from India.
   _____
5 Where are **Maggie and Jake Gyllenhaal** from?
   _____
6 How old are **you and your friend**?
   _____

2 Choose the correct words to complete the questions and sentences.

1 We *'s not* / *'re not* doctors.
2 *Is* / *Are* Ismail from Turkey?
3 Sam and I *am* / *are* in London.
4 I *'m not* / *'re not* your teacher.
5 Where *is* / *are* the actor from?
6 Ana and Rosa *is* / *are* from Spain.

◀ Go back to page 11

96

GRAMMAR PRACTICE

2A Singular and plural nouns

We use *a* and *an* with singular nouns. We use *a* with nouns that start with consonants (*b*, *d*, *f*, *g*, etc.) and we use *an* with nouns that start with vowels (*a*, *e*, *i*, *o*, *u*).

It's a book.   She's an actor.

To make a noun plural, we usually add *-s* or *-es*.

a key ⇨ three keys   a watch ⇨ two watches

▶ 2.3	Singular	Plural
	It's **an** umbrella.	They're umbrella**s**.
	I'm **a** waitress.	We're waitress**es**.

Spelling rules for plurals

We usually add *-s* to nouns to make a plural.

bag ⇨ bags

When a noun ends in a consonant + **y**, we remove the **y** and then add *-ies*.

country ⇨ countries

When a noun ends in **ch**, **sh**, **s**, or **x**, we add *-es*.

watch ⇨ watches

Some plurals are irregular.

child ⇨ children   man ⇨ men   woman ⇨ women   person ⇨ people

1 Complete the sentences with singular or plural nouns and *a* or *an*, if necessary.

Singular	Plural
1 It's a city.	They're _____ .
2 She's _____ .	They're actors.
3 Are you a waitress?	Are you _____ ?
4 He's not _____ .	They're not children.
5 It's a watch.	They're _____ .
6 It's not _____ .	They're not umbrellas.
7 I'm a woman.	We're _____ .
8 He's _____ .	They're people.

2 Match the parts to make sentences and questions.

1 Alice is an _____	**a** tour guide.
2 It's an _____	**b** IT worker.
3 He's a _____	**c** umbrella.
4 Jo and I are _____	**d** engineers.
5 Are you a _____	**e** sunglasses?
6 Where are my _____	**f** chef?

◀ Go back to page 14

2A *this, that, these, those*

We use *this* and *these* + the verb *be* to identify things that are near us.

This is my purse and these are my sunglasses.

We use *that* and *those* + the verb *be* to identify things that are not near us.

That's my school and those are my friends.

▶ 2.4	Things that are near	Things that are not near
Singular	**This** is my wallet.	**That**'s my teacher.
Plural	**These** are my books.	**Those** are my classmates.

> **Look!** We can also use *this/that/these/those* + noun. *That book is new.*

1 Choose the correct words to complete the sentences.

1 *This / These* is my room.
2 Excuse me. Are *that / those* your glasses?
3 Look! Is *this / that* your phone over there?
4 Are *these / this* your keys?
5 Is *that / those* your pen, or is it my pen?
6 Are *these / this* your credit cards?

◀ Go back to page 15

2C Possessive adjectives, *'s* for possession

We use possessive adjectives before nouns to say that something belongs to someone.

Joseph is my brother.   This is our house.

We use the same possessive adjectives for singular and plural nouns.

Is that your key?   Are those your keys?

▶ 2.11	Possessive adjectives
my	I'm French. **My** wife is Spanish.
your	Are **you** sad? **Your** boyfriend's not here.
his	**He**'s a teacher. **His** students are young.
her	**She**'s an actor. **Her** house is big.
its	**It**'s a small restaurant. **Its** pizzas are good.
our	**We**'re late. **Our** boss isn't happy.
their	**They**'re tour guides. **Their** jobs are interesting.

If we talk about possession with a name or a noun, we add *'s* to the name or noun.

Is that the teacher's book?   Are you Rob's sister?

1 Complete the sentences with the correct possessive adjectives.

1 Hello. _____ name's Kate.
2 We're from Lima. This is a photo of _____ house.
3 He's French. _____ name is Olivier.
4 They're British, but _____ parents are from Peru.
5 Hi, I'm Tom. What's _____ name?
6 This is Luisa and _____ husband, Sven.

2 Complete the sentences with *'s* for possession so they mean the same as the first sentences.

1 She's Olivia. Those are her sunglasses.
   Those are *Olivia's sunglasses* .
2 He's my son. That's his credit card.
   That's _____ .
3 This is my daughter. Her name is Ruby.
   My _____ .
4 She's our doctor. Her phone number is 665342.
   Our _____ .

◀ Go back to page 19

97

GRAMMAR PRACTICE

3A Simple present (*I, you, we, they*)

We use the simple present to talk about facts and routines.

I drink coffee for breakfast.
We eat a lot of fruit.

We form negatives with *don't* (*do not*) + the base form of the verb (*eat, have, play, ...*).

My parents don't like tea.
They don't eat meat.

We form questions with *do* + subject + the base form of the verb.

Do you like fish?
Do they have breakfast?

▶ 3.3 **I / you / we / they**

+	I **have** a big breakfast. You **eat** a lot of fruit.
−	We **don't drink** coffee. They **don't like** cheese.
?	**Do** you **have** a big breakfast? **Do** they **eat** fish?
Y/N	Yes, I **do**. / No, I **don't**. Yes, they **do**. / No, they **don't**.

1 Complete the sentences with the correct form of the verbs in parentheses.

1 I _____ pizza. (like)
2 We _____ eggs or cheese. (not eat)
3 They _____ lunch at home. (not have)
4 You _____ tea. (drink)
5 Our children _____ green vegetables. (not like)
6 My husband and I _____ a lot of fruit. (eat)
7 I _____ coffee at night. (not drink)
8 You _____ breakfast. (not have)

2 Order the words to make questions. Then complete the short answers.

1 you / meat / eat / do
_____ ? No, I _____ .
2 you / do / food / like / Indian
_____ ? Yes, we _____ .
3 potatoes / they / like / do
_____ ? Yes, they _____ .
4 drink / do / you and Anna / coffee
_____ ? No, we _____ .

◀ Go back to page 25

3C Simple present (*he, she, it*)

For *he*, *she* and *it*, we often add *-s* to the base form to make the affirmative form.

I drink tea for breakfast. ⇨ *He drinks tea for breakfast.*

Spelling rules for simple present verbs with *he, she, it*

We usually add *-s* to the base form.
work ⇨ *works*

When a verb ends in a consonant + *y*, we remove the *y* and then add *-ies*.
study ⇨ *studies*

When a verb ends in *ch*, *sh*, *s*, or *x*, we add *-es*.
watch ⇨ *watches*

Some verbs are irregular.
go ⇨ *goes*   *do* ⇨ *does*   *have* ⇨ *has*

We form negatives with *doesn't* (*does not*) + the base form of the verb.

My sister doesn't speak English.

We form questions with *does* + subject + the base form of the verb.

Does our teacher work on weekends?

▶ 3.14 **he / she / it**

+	Kevin **exercises** in the morning. She **lives** in Boston.
−	He **doesn't want** a new car. My house **doesn't have** a yard.
?	**Does** he **live** in Chicago? **Does** Sandra **go** to the gym?
Y/N	Yes, he **does**. / No, he **doesn't**. Yes, she **does**. / No, she **doesn't**.

1 Write the simple present *he*, *she*, *it* form of the verbs.

1 like _____   5 go _____
2 have _____   6 try _____
3 play _____   7 drink _____
4 eat _____   8 wash _____

2 Rewrite the sentences. Use affirmative (+), negative (−) or question (?) forms.

1 My father makes good cakes.
_____ (?)
2 Anna doesn't go to college.
_____ (+)
3 Mark works on Tuesdays.
_____ (−)
4 Does she have two children?
_____ (+)
5 Sam thinks about soccer all day.
_____ (?)
6 My sister doesn't watch TV in the evening.
_____ (+)

◀ Go back to page 29

GRAMMAR PRACTICE

4A Frequency adverbs

We use frequency adverbs with the simple present to talk about routines.

They always go to the gym on Friday.
I sometimes play soccer on the weekend.

Frequency adverbs come before most verbs, but we put frequency adverbs after the verb *be*.

I usually have lunch at work.
I'm always at home in the evening. **NOT** *I always am at home in the evening.*

▶ 4.3	Frequency adverbs	
always	He **always** takes a shower in the morning.	100%
usually	Julia **usually** gets up early.	
often	You **often** get home after 9:00 p.m.	
sometimes	I'm **sometimes** late for class.	
never	My parents **never** drink coffee.	0%

Look! *never* has a negative meaning, but we use a affirmative form.
My children never get up early. **NOT** *My children don't never get up early.*

4C Simple present: *wh-* questions

We ask questions with question words to ask for specific information.

A day / time of day – *When does your brother go to the gym?*
A time – *What time does the class start?*
A thing – *What do you drink at work?*
A person – *Who do you work with?*
A place – *Where do you live?*
A reason – *Why do you get up early on Saturday?*
A number – *How many keys do you have?*
An age – *How old is Julian?*
A manner – *How do you get to work?*

The word order in questions with most verbs is question word + *do/does* + subject + main verb + rest of question.

▶ 4.8	Question word	*do/does*	Subject	Main verb	Rest of question
	What	do	you	have	for breakfast?
	When	does	she	see	her friends?
	Where	do	his parents	work?	

With the verb *be*, the word order in questions is question word + *am/is/are* + subject + rest of question.

▶ 4.9	Question word	*am/is/are*	Subject	Rest of question
	Why	am	I	cold?
	What time	is	the bus?	
	How	are	you	today?

1 Order the words to make sentences.

1 brother / never / my / up / gets / early
_____ .

2 office / I / have / usually / lunch / at / the
_____ .

3 trains / late / always / the / night / at / are
_____ .

4 always / the / morning / a / take / I / in / shower
_____ .

5 dressed / I / get / usually / breakfast / before
_____ .

6 friendly / very / is / teacher / my / always
_____ .

7 never / we / dinner / before / have / 9:00 p.m.
_____ .

8 videos / watch / sometimes / in / we / class
_____ .

◀ Go back to page 33

1 Complete the questions with the question words in the box.

How many   What   What time
When   Where   Why

1 _____ does your brother do?
   He's a taxi driver.
2 _____ do you usually play tennis?
   I usually play on the weekend.
3 _____ does your sister work?
   She works at the hospital.
4 _____ do you like your job?
   Because I meet a lot of people and it's interesting.
5 _____ does your English class start?
   At 7:30 p.m.
6 _____ cousins do you have?
   I have eight cousins.

2 Write questions.

1 What / you / want for dinner?
_____

2 Why / she / ride her bike to work?
_____

3 Who / be / your favorite actors?
_____

4 How / they / know that man?
_____

5 Where / your brother / go grocery shopping?
_____

6 What time / the lesson / finish?
_____

◀ Go back to page 37

99

GRAMMAR PRACTICE

5A *can* and *can't*

We use *can* and *can't* (*cannot*) to talk about ability.
I can play the piano.   My grandmother can't drive.
To make questions with *can*, we put *can* before the subject.
Can you speak Portuguese?   What can he cook?
We use the same form for all people and things.
I/You/He/She/It/We/They can swim.

▶ 5.3	I / you / he / she / it / we / they
+	I **can speak** Italian.
–	You **can't play** the violin.
?	**Can** he **cook** Chinese food?
Y/N	Yes, he **can**. / No, he **can't**.

Look! We use *can/can't* with *well* to say we are good/bad at something.
She can speak English well.
They can't swim well.

1 Write affirmative (+) or negative (–) sentences with *can*.
   1 My sister / drive. (–)
   _____
   2 Dogs / swim. (+)
   _____
   3 Her son / use a computer. (–)
   _____
   4 My dad / cook well. (+)
   _____

2 Complete the questions. Use *can* and the verbs in brackets. Then write the short answers.
   1 A _____ Sarah _____ five kilometers? (run)
     B Yes, _____ .
   2 A _____ you and Jo _____ salsa? (dance)
     B No, _____ .
   3 A _____ your son _____ Italian food? (cook)
     B Yes, _____ .
   4 A _____ you _____ well? (sing)
     B No, _____ .

◀ Go back to page 43

5C Object pronouns

The object of a sentence is the noun which comes after the verb.
I like cookies. (*cookies* are the object of the sentence)
Ana calls her sister every week. (*her sister* is the object of the sentence)
We use object pronouns instead of nouns when we know what the noun is.
Emily is a really nice person. I like her. (*her* = Emily)
Fruit juice is good for you. I drink it for breakfast. (*it* = fruit juice)

▶ 5.14	Subject pronouns	Object pronouns	
	I	me	I'm here. Can you see **me**?
	you	you	You're friendly. I like **you**.
	he	him	Paul's a doctor. We work with **him**.
	she	her	Who is Karen? I don't know **her**.
	it	it	I love hiking. Do you like **it**?
	we	us	We're at work. Call **us** if you have a problem.
	you	you	You and Ben are only 12 years old. Your parents take care of **you**.
	they	them	I have three cats. I love **them**!

Look! We always use object pronouns, not subject pronouns, after prepositions.
Can you come with me?
Where's Paul? I want to talk to him.

1 Replace the underlined words with object pronouns.

   1 I love <u>books</u>.   _____
   2 My sister has <u>the car</u>.   _____
   3 He doesn't like <u>Maria</u>.   _____
   4 They cook for <u>my wife and me</u>.   _____
   5 Give the book to <u>John</u>.   _____
   6 Can he help <u>you and Abdul</u>?   _____

2 Choose the correct words to complete the sentences.
   1 Ivan's a waiter. I see *he* / *him* at work.
   2 Lucy lives in France, but *she* / *her* isn't French.
   3 I hate cleaning. Why do I do *me* / *it*?
   4 Your children are quiet. Where are *they* / *them*?
   5 This bike is very fast. Do you want *it* / *them*?
   6 Can you take care of my plant? *It* / *Her* needs water every day.

◀ Go back to page 47

GRAMMAR PRACTICE

6A *there is/are*

We use *there's* (*there is*) + *a/an* with singular nouns to say that something exists.

There's a beautiful park near my house.   *There's an umbrella on the table.*

We use *there are* with plural nouns to say that something exists.

There are five hotels in my city.   *There are six people on the bus.*

We often use *some* in affirmative sentences with plural nouns. We use *any* in negative sentences and questions with plural nouns.

There are some good stores downtown.   *There aren't any museums.*
Are there any hotels near here?

We can also make negative sentences with *no*:

There's no museum.   *There are no museums.*

6.2	Singular	Plural
+	There's a school. There's an airport.	There are some schools. There are two airports.
–	There's no theater.	There aren't any / There are no theaters.
?	Is there a restaurant?	Are there any restaurants?
Y/N	Yes, there is. / No, there isn't. No, there's not.	Yes, there are. / No, there aren't.

1 Complete the sentences with the correct forms of *there is/are*.

1 _____ a great museum in town.
2 _____ a school near your house?
3 I'm sorry, but _____ no drugstore near here.
4 _____ some cheap hotels near the train station.
5 _____ any parks, so children play in the street.
6 _____ any good restaurants at the shopping mall?

2 Complete the sentences with *a/an*, *some* or *any*.

1 There aren't _____ supermarkets in this area.
2 There's _____ good hospital near here.
3 There are _____ police officers in the street.
4 There isn't _____ Italian restaurant in our town.
5 Are there _____ pens in your purse?
6 Is there _____ police station near here?

◀ Go back to page 51

6C Prepositions of place

We use prepositions of place to say where an object or person is.

There's a table next to the bed.   *Your keys are behind the sofa.*
My brother is in the kitchen.   *Simon is next to Amy.*

6.9 Prepositions of place

on	 The phone is **on** the table.	next to	 The chair is **next to** the table.
in	 The phone is **in** the purse.	in front of	 The table is **in front of** the chair.
above	 The shelves are **above** the table.	between	 The chair is **between** the window and the table.
under	 The purse is **under** the table.	behind	 The lamp is **behind** the sofa.

1 Look at the picture. Write sentences saying where the things are with prepositions of place.

1 refrigerator / stove
_____
2 shelves / bed
_____
3 cat / table
_____
4 laptop / desk
_____
5 window / sofa
_____
6 table / sofa
_____

◀ Go back to page 55

101

GRAMMAR PRACTICE

7A Simple past: be

We use the simple past of the verb *be* to talk about situations in the past.

Marilyn Monroe was an actor. She was American.

The affirmative simple past forms of the verb *be* are *was* and *were*.

I was in New York yesterday. The people were very friendly.

The negative simple past forms of the verb *be* are *wasn't* (*was not*) and *weren't* (*were not*).

I wasn't at home last night.
The Beatles weren't from Manchester.

We form questions with *was/were* + subject.

Was the teacher late for class?
Were you cold at work today?

▶ 7.2	I / he / she / it	you / we / they
+	I **was** happy.	They **were** singers.
–	It **wasn't** a good movie.	We **weren't** at home yesterday.
?	**Was** she at school?	**Were** they Mexican?
Y/N	Yes, she **was**. / No, she **wasn't**.	Yes, they **were**. / No, they **weren't**.

1 Choose the correct words to complete the sentences.
 1 My father *was / were* an artist.
 2 Enrique and Javier *wasn't / weren't* at work on Monday.
 3 How *was / were* your vacation?
 4 This book *wasn't / weren't* very interesting.
 5 My grandparents *was / were* both musicians.
 6 What *was / were* the answer to this question?
 7 *Were / Was* you and your sister at home yesterday?
 8 We *wasn't / weren't* happy with our grades.

2 Complete the conversations with the correct form of *was* or *were*.
 1 A _____ you at home yesterday?
   B No, I _____ . I _____ at the hospital.
 2 A _____ the movie good?
   B Yes, it _____ . The actors _____ amazing.
 3 A _____ your parents teachers?
   B No, they _____ . They _____ writers.
 4 A _____ Akira Kurosawa a photographer?
   B No, he _____ . He _____ a movie director.
 5 A _____ you late for school today?
   B Yes, I _____ . I _____ 30 minutes late.
 6 A _____ you and Nico at the same school?
   B Yes, we _____ , but we _____ in the same class.

◀ Go back to page 61

7C Simple past: regular verbs

We use the simple past to talk about completed actions in the past. We usually add *-ed* to the base form to form the simple past of regular verbs.

cook ⇨ cooked   *I cooked pasta yesterday.*

Spelling rules for regular affirmative simple past verbs

We usually add **-ed** to the base form.
cook ⇨ cooked

When a verb ends in **-e**, we add **-d**.
dance ⇨ danced

When a verb ends in consonant + **y**, we change the **y** to **i** and then we add **-ed**.
study ⇨ studied

When a verb ends in vowel + consonant, we usually double the consonant and add **-ed**.
stop ⇨ stopped

We form the negative with *didn't* (*did not*) + base form.

I didn't want coffee for breakfast.   *My parents didn't like the food.*

We form questions with *did* + subject + base form.

Did she play the piano yesterday?   *Did your brother live in Canada?*

▶ 7.12	I / you / he / she / it / we / they
+	He **worked** in Washington.
–	They **didn't live** in this house.
?	**Did** you **study** Spanish in college?
Y/N	Yes, I **did**. / No, I **didn't**.

1 Rewrite the sentences and questions in the simple past.

 1 My grandfather lives on this street.
  _____
 2 I cook paella for lunch.
  _____
 3 She doesn't ride her bike home.
  _____
 4 The train doesn't stop in Paris.
  _____
 5 Liam studies science in college.
  _____
 6 Does she dance with her friends?
  _____
 7 Do they live in Ecuador?
  _____
 8 Elise doesn't want ice cream.
  _____

◀ Go back to page 65

GRAMMAR PRACTICE

8A Simple past: irregular verbs

A lot of common verbs have an irregular simple past form (for a full list of irregular verbs see page 151).

take ⇨ took   I took a taxi to the airport.
go ⇨ went   We went to the park yesterday.
buy ⇨ bought I bought a new purse.

Only the affirmative forms are irregular. We form the negative with *didn't* + base form.

We didn't take the train.
They didn't go to the party.
My sister didn't buy coffee.

We form questions with *did* + subject + base form.

Did they take the train?
Did you go to the grocery store?
Did we buy any vegetables?

▶ 8.2	I / you / he / she / it / we / they
+	He **went** to college in Boston.
−	She **didn't have** breakfast yesterday.
?	**Did** you **see** Carly at the party?
Y/N	Yes, I **did**. / No, I **didn't**.

1 Complete the sentences with the simple past form of the verbs in parentheses.

1 They _____ to work by car. (go)
2 She _____ to Hong Kong. (fly)
3 I _____ on the 11:30 bus to Newcastle. (get)
4 Paula _____ her daughter a lot of stories. (tell)
5 Richard _____ coffee and toast for breakfast. (have)
6 Clarissa _____ "Hi". (say)
7 I _____ pasta for dinner. (make)
8 My mom _____ to work yesterday. (drive)

2 Complete the questions and answers with the correct form of the verbs in parentheses.

1 A What time _____ her train _____ ? (leave)
  B It _____ at 8:00 p.m.
2 A _____ you _____ a dress to the party? (wear)
  B No, I _____ a dress. I _____ jeans.
3 A _____ he _____ a bus to the station? (take)
  B No, he _____ a bus. He _____ the subway.
4 A _____ you _____ well last night? (sleep)
  B No, I _____ at all!
5 A _____ you _____ a big lunch? (have)
  B No, I _____ . I _____ a sandwich.
6 A _____ you _____ to your dad yesterday? (speak)
  B No, but I _____ to my mom.

◀ Go back to page 69

8C *there was/were*

We use *there was* and *a/an* with singular nouns to say that something existed in the past.

There was a big school here 50 years ago.
There was an egg in the refrigerator yesterday.

We use *there were* with plural nouns to say that something existed in the past.

There were lots of fields here in the past.
There were two books on my desk.

We often use *some* in affirmative sentences with plural nouns. We use *any* in negative sentences and questions. We can also use *no* with a singular or plural noun after *there was/were*.

There were some people in the store.
There weren't any children. / There were no children.
Were there any cakes in the grocery store?

▶ 8.9	Singular	Plural
+	**There was** a road. **There was** an old house.	**There were** two stores. **There were some** trees.
−	**There was no** library. / **There wasn't** a library.	**There were no** restaurants. / **There weren't any** restaurants.
?	**Was there** a school?	**Were there any** tall buildings?
Y/N	Yes, **there was**. / No, **there wasn't**.	Yes, **there were**. / No, **there weren't**.

1 Look at the picture of Fairfield 100 years ago. Complete the sentences with the correct form of *there was/were* and *a/an* or *some/any/no*.

1 _____ tall buildings, but _____ stores.
2 _____ cars in the town, but _____ bicycles.
3 _____ movie theater, but _____ club.
4 _____ old tree and _____ flowers.

◀ Go back to page 73

GRAMMAR PRACTICE

9A Present continuous

We use the present continuous to talk about actions that are happening now. We often use time expressions like *right now* and *at the moment* with the present continuous.

I'm wearing my new jeans today.
We're not working at the moment.
What are you doing now?

We form the present continuous with the verb *be* + the *-ing* form of the main verb.

Spelling rules for the *-ing* form

We usually add *-ing* to the base form of the verb.
cook ⇨ cooking   watch ⇨ watching

When the verb ends in a consonant + *e*, we usually remove the *e* and then add *-ing*.
take ⇨ taking   dance ⇨ dancing

When the verb ends in a consonant + a vowel + a consonant, we double the consonant and then add *-ing*.
begin ⇨ beginning   get ⇨ getting

▶ 9.3	I	he / she / it	you / we / they
+	I**'m listening** to music.	He**'s reading** a book.	You**'re singing**.
−	I**'m not watching** TV.	She**'s not working**.	We**'re not stopping** here.
?	**Am** I **sleeping**?	**Is** he **studying**?	**Are** they **going**?
Y/N	Yes, I **am**. / No, I**'m not**.	Yes, he **is**. / No, he**'s not**. / No, he **isn't**.	Yes, they **are**. / No, they**'re not**.

1 Write the *-ing* form of the verbs.
  1 buy _____   6 look _____
  2 drive _____   7 make _____
  3 sit _____   8 stop _____
  4 go _____   9 swim _____
  5 leave _____   10 watch _____

2 Write affirmative (+) sentences, negative (−) sentences or questions (?) in the present continuous.
  1 George / listen to / music / now (+)
  _____
  2 you / wear / a new coat (?)
  _____
  3 she / listen to / me (−)
  _____
  4 they / do / their homework (−)
  _____
  5 we / have dinner / at the moment (+)
  _____
  6 it / rain / today (?)
  _____

◀ Go back to page 79

9C *How often* + expressions of frequency

We use *How often ... ?* + the simple present or the verb *be* to ask about frequency.

How often do you go shopping?
How often does Tim go to London?
How often are you late for class?

We can answer the question *How often ...?* with expressions of frequency.

How often are your English classes?
I have a class once or twice a week. (*once* = one time, *twice* = two times)

▶ 9.13	**Expressions of frequency**
every day/week/month/year	I go to the gym **every day**.
once a day/week/month/year	John has a vacation **once a year**.
twice a day/week/month/year	Ali has a coffee with his friends **twice a week**.
three/four times a day/week/month/year	They play soccer **three or four times a month**.

Look! We can also answer questions with *How often ...?* with frequency adverbs (*always, usually, often, sometimes, never*).
How often do you walk to work?
I never walk to work. I usually get the bus.

1 Complete the questions and answers. Use the words in parentheses.

  1 How often _____ your bike? (you / ride)
    I _____ my bike _____ day.
  2 How often _____ in your city? (it / snow)
    It only _____ once _____ year.
  3 How often _____ his grandparents? (Luis / see)
    He _____ his grandparents three _____ a month.
  4 How often _____ tennis? (you / play)
    We _____ tennis _____ weekend.
  5 How often _____ their friends? (they / meet)
    They _____ their friends twice _____ week.

◀ Go back to page 83

GRAMMAR PRACTICE

10A Present continuous for future plans

We use the present continuous to talk about plans and arrangements in the future (for spelling rules of -ing forms see page 104).

I'm going to the dentist next week.

▶ 10.3	I	he / she / it	you / we / they
+	I'm meeting friends tonight.	She's taking the bus tomorrow.	You're working next Tuesday.
–	I'm not going to school tomorrow.	He's not watching a movie tonight.	We're not playing tennis later.
?	Am I working this weekend?	Is she staying home tonight?	Are they going to the gym?
Y/N	Yes, I am. / No, I'm not.	Yes, she is. / No, she's not.	Yes, they are. / No, they're not.

We often use a future time expression to talk about future plans and arrangements. Time expressions usually go at the end of the sentence.

▶ 10.4	Future time expressions
this morning/afternoon/evening	We're taking the train **this afternoon**.
tonight	What are you having for dinner **tonight**?
tomorrow	Sven isn't coming to the party **tomorrow**.
next week/month/year	We're going on vacation **next week**.
later	Are you meeting Jorge **later**?

1 Complete the sentences and questions with the present continuous form of the verbs in the box.

> take   not visit   meet
> not come   stay   watch

1 We _____ our friends for dinner later.
2 _____ you _____ the soccer game tonight?
3 They _____ the 7:30 train to Edinburgh tomorrow.
4 He _____ with some friends in Lima at the weekend.
5 Maria is sick. She _____ to the concert this evening.
6 We _____ the museum next week. It's closed.

2 Write sentences and questions in the present continuous.

1 I / meet / my friends this weekend
   _____ .
2 My brother / not visit / us this month
   _____ .
3 They / not go / on vacation this summer
   _____ .
4 What / you / cook / for dinner on Saturday
   _____ ?

◀ Go back to page 87

10C Question review

Questions can be *yes/no* questions or they can ask for specific information with a question word (*where*, *when*, *who*, etc.).

Do you live in Japan?   Yes, I do. / No, I don't.
Where are you from?   I'm from Turkey.

For most verbs, the word order in questions is: (question word +) auxiliary verb + subject + base form of main verb + rest of question.

▶ 10.12	(Question word)	Auxiliary verb	Subject	Main verb	Rest of question
Simple present		Does	Chris	speak	English?
	What	do	you	have	for breakfast?
Simple past		Did	Lucy	call	you yesterday?
	When	did	you	arrive	at the airport?
Present continuous		Is	it	snowing	now?
	Where	are	they	going	next week?

For the verbs *be* and *can*, the word order in questions is: (question word +) verb + subject + rest of question.

▶ 10.13	(Question word)	Verb	Subject	Rest of question
be (simple present)		Is	Julia	here?
	Where	are	you	from?
be (simple past)		Were	you	late for work?
	Who	was	Philip	with?
can		Can	you	ride a motorcycle?
	What sports	can	they	play?

1 Order the words to make questions.

1 rock climbing / does / go / how often / he
   _____ ?
2 you / what / for / lunch / are / having
   _____ ?
3 homework / when / she / did / do / her
   _____ ?
4 can / instrument / you / play / an
   _____ ?
5 you / crying / why / are
   _____ ?
6 did / where / he / on / go / vacation
   _____ ?
7 they / were / home / night / last / at
   _____ ?
8 what / is / she / time / leaving
   _____ ?

◀ Go back to page 91

VOCABULARY PRACTICE

Hello Classroom language

1 ▶ 1.7 Listen and repeat.

1 Open your books.　　2 Close your books.　　3 Turn to page 5.　　4 Look at the picture.

5 Listen and repeat.　　6 Work in pairs.　　7 Excuse me, what does "nice" mean?　　8 I'm sorry, I don't understand.

9 How do you say "bom dia" in English?　　10 Can you repeat that, please?　　11 How do you spell that?　　12 Sorry I'm late.

2 Complete the conversation with the words in the box.

turn　open　listen　~~late~~　look　spell　work　close　mean　repeat

Norio Hello. Sorry I'm ¹ _late_ .
Teacher Hello. Are you Norio?
Norio Yes, I am.
Teacher I'm your teacher. My name's Helen.
Norio Hi.
Teacher ² _____ your book and turn to page 6, please.
Norio I'm sorry, can you ³ _____ that?
Teacher Yes. ⁴ _____ to page 6 in your book.
Norio OK.

Teacher ⁵ _____ at the picture of a family.
Norio Excuse me, what does "family" ⁶ _____ ?
Teacher Your mother, father, brothers, sisters ...
Norio I understand. How do you ⁷ _____ "family"?
Teacher F-A-M-I-L-Y.
Norio Thank you.
Teacher ⁸ _____ and repeat – "family".
Norio Family.
Teacher Very good. Now, ⁹ _____ your books and ¹⁰ _____ in pairs ...

◀ Go back to page 5

VOCABULARY PRACTICE

1A Countries and nationalities

1 ▶ 1.12 Listen and repeat.

1 Argentina / Argentinian
2 Brazil / Brazilian
3 Canada / Canadian
4 Chile / Chilean
5 China / Chinese
6 Colombia / Colombian
7 France / French
8 Germany / German
9 India / Indian
10 Italy / Italian
11 Japan / Japanese
12 Mexico / Mexican
13 Peru / Peruvian
14 Russia / Russian
15 Spain / Spanish
16 Turkey / Turkish
17 the UK / British
18 the U.S. / American

2 Look at the pictures. Complete the sentences with the correct country or nationality.

1 Lionel Messi is _____ .

2 Paris is in _____ .

3 A kimono comes from _____ .

4 Pasta is _____ food.

5 A panda is an animal from _____ .

6 Washington, D.C., is the capital of _____ .

7 Machu Picchu is in _____ .

8 These are _____ dolls.

9 The Taj Mahal is in _____ .

10 Rio de Janeiro is a _____ city.

◀ Go back to page 6

107

VOCABULARY PRACTICE

1B Jobs

1 ▶ 1.19 Listen and repeat.

1 an actor

2 a chef

3 a doctor

4 an engineer

5 an IT worker

6 an office worker

7 a police officer

8 a receptionist

9 a salesclerk

10 a singer

11 a student

12 a taxi driver

13 a teacher

14 a tour guide

15 a TV host

16 a waiter/a waitress

Look! We use *an* with jobs that begin with vowels (*a, e, i, o, u*) and *a* with jobs that begin with consonants (*b, c, d, f,* etc.).
I'm **a** teacher.
Are you **an** office worker?

2 Match the jobs in the box with objects 1–8. Use *a* or *an*.

waiter   salesclerk   engineer   singer   receptionist   doctor   chef   actor

1 _____

2 _____

3 _____

4 _____

5 _____

6 _____

7 _____

8 _____

◀ Go back to page 8

VOCABULARY PRACTICE

1C Adjectives (1)

1 ▶ 1.32 Listen and repeat.

1 good   2 bad   3 beautiful   4 ugly   5 big   6 small
7 cheap   8 expensive   9 interesting   10 boring   11 new   12 old
13 happy   14 sad   15 easy   16 difficult   17 old   18 young

2 Choose the correct words to complete the conversations.

A This phone is ¹cheap / boring. It's only $50.
B Yes, but it's not ²difficult / good. Look at this phone.
A It's $795! It's very ³expensive / new.

A How ⁶good / old is Michael?
B He's ⁷new / young. He's three years old today!
A He's very ⁸happy / sad.

A Hi, Sara. Do you understand Italian?
B Yes. I'm Spanish, but Italian is ⁴big / easy for me.
A Oh, that's ⁵interesting / ugly.

A Wow – this painting is ⁹beautiful / difficult!
B Yes, but it's very ¹⁰bad / small.
A My house is small, too!

◀ Go back to page 11

109

> VOCABULARY PRACTICE

2A Personal items

1 ▶ 2.2 Listen and repeat.

 1 a backpack
 2 a book
 3 a camera
 4 a cell phone
 5 a change purse

 6 a credit card
 7 glasses
 8 keys
 9 a pen
 10 a pencil

 11 a purse
 12 a tablet
 13 an umbrella
 14 a wallet
 15 a watch

2 Write the items you can see in the pictures.

1 _____   4 _____
2 _____   5 _____
3 _____   6 _____

◀ Go back to page 14

2B Colors

1 ▶ 2.8 Listen and repeat.

 1 black
 2 blue
 3 brown
 4 gold
 5 gray

 6 green
  7 orange
 8 pink
9 purple

 10 red
11 silver
 12 white
13 yellow

2 Write the colors.

1 red + blue = _____   4 black + white = _____
2 red + white = _____   5 red + yellow = _____
3 blue + yellow = _____ 6 red + blue + yellow = _____

◀ Go back to page 16

VOCABULARY PRACTICE

1C Numbers 0–100

1 ▶ 1.26 Listen and repeat.

0 zero	5 five	10 ten	15 fifteen	20 twenty	50 fifty	100 a hundred/
1 one	6 six	11 eleven	16 sixteen	21 twenty-one	60 sixty	one hundred
2 two	7 seven	12 twelve	17 seventeen	22 twenty-two	70 seventy
3 three	8 eight	13 thirteen	18 eighteen	30 thirty	80 eighty
4 four	9 nine	14 fourteen	19 nineteen	40 forty	90 ninety

2 Write the numbers as words or digits.

1 34 _____   3 63 _____   5 88 _____   7 29 _____   9 12 _____
2 _____ seventy-two   4 _____ ninety-one   6 _____ fifty-seven   8 _____ forty-four   10 _____ a hundred

◀ Go back to page 10

2C Family and friends

1 ▶ 2.10 Listen and repeat.

1 grandfather 2 grandmother   4 mother   5 father   7 son   8 daughter
3 grandparents   6 parents   9 children

10 husband   11 wife   12 sister   13 brother   14 boyfriend   15 girlfriend

2 Look at the family tree. Read the sentences and write the names.

1 My brother is Liam. _____
2 Julia is my wife. _____
3 My sister is Julia, and my brother is George. _____
4 My girlfriend is Molly. _____
5 My parents are George and Gloria, and my sister is Molly. _____
6 Bob is my father, and Mark and George are my brothers. _____
7 My wife is Judith. _____
8 My husband's brother is Mark. _____
9 Our children are Julia, Mark, and George.
   _____ and _____
10 Our parents are Judith and Bob.
   _____, _____ and _____

◀ Go back to page 18

111

VOCABULARY PRACTICE

3A Food and drink

1 ▶ 3.2 Listen and repeat.

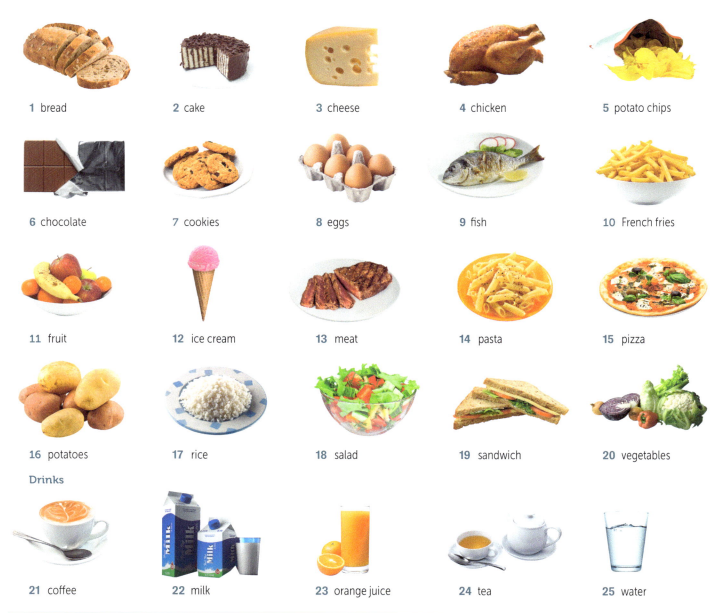

Food

1 bread
2 cake
3 cheese
4 chicken
5 potato chips
6 chocolate
7 cookies
8 eggs
9 fish
10 French fries
11 fruit
12 ice cream
13 meat
14 pasta
15 pizza
16 potatoes
17 rice
18 salad
19 sandwich
20 vegetables

Drinks

21 coffee
22 milk
23 orange juice
24 tea
25 water

Look! If we want to talk about the food and drink that we eat and drink at breakfast, lunch, and dinner, we can use the verb *have*.
What do you **have** *for breakfast/lunch/dinner?*
I **have** *coffee for breakfast. I* **have** *a sandwich for lunch. I* **have** *fish for dinner.*

8:00 a.m. — have breakfast
1:00 p.m. — have lunch
6:30 p.m. — have dinner

2 Choose the correct words to complete the sentences.

1 Ice cream has *milk / cheese* in it.
2 Potatoes are *fruit / vegetables*.
3 Cake, cookies, and *chocolate / salad* are bad for you.
4 Chips and French fries come from *potatoes / pasta*.
5 British people have *rice / milk* in their tea.
6 Spaghetti is a type of *bread / pasta*.
7 I have *breakfast / lunch* at 8:00 a.m.
8 Vegetarians don't eat *meat / salad*.
9 I drink *orange juice / fish* in the morning.
10 I have *chocolate / meat* and vegetables for dinner.

112 ◀ Go back to page 24

VOCABULARY PRACTICE

3C Common verbs (1)

1 ▶ 3.12 Listen and repeat.

1 **exchange** money

2 **exercise**

3 **go** to school

4 **have** two children

5 **know** the answer

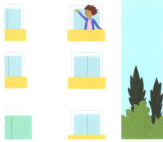
6 **live** in an apartment

7 **make** coffee

8 **say** "goodbye"

9 **study** German

10 **think** (about …)

11 **use** a tablet

12 **want** a drink

13 **watch** a movie

14 **work** in an office

Look! We use *make* for food and drink:
I make a sandwich every day.
We make dinner for our friends.

We use *think* for thoughts and opinions:
I think about work. (thought)
We think it's a good idea. (opinion)

2 Choose the correct words to complete the sentences.

1 After work, I *know / go / use* to the gym.
2 I *study / say / live* English and Spanish in college.
3 I *make / do / work* dinner for my family every evening.
4 I *think / know / work* in a restaurant – I'm a waitress!
5 A Do you like that book?
   B No, I *think / watch / use* it's boring.
6 My boyfriend and I *watch / say / live* TV in the evening.
7 Do you *exchange / exercise / study* at the gym?
8 Do they *use / know / live* in a big house?
9 I *study / live / say* "good morning" to people at work.
10 My cell phone is old. I *watch / want / work* a new one.
11 A What's the capital of China?
    B I don't *go / use / know*.
12 My children *use / say / make* the Internet a lot.

◀ Go back to page 28

113

VOCABULARY PRACTICE

4A Daily routine verbs

1 ▶ 4.2 Listen and repeat.

1 get up

2 take a shower

3 get dressed

4 leave home

5 start work

6 go grocery shopping

7 listen to the radio

8 do housework / do homework

9 finish work

10 get home

11 go to bed

12 read a book

2 Complete the text with the correct form of the verbs in the box.

do (x2)   get (x3)   go (x2)   leave   finish   listen   start   take

I'm Miranda, and this is my typical day. I [1]_____ up at 7:00 in the morning and [2]_____ a shower. Then I have breakfast with my son, Leon. He [3]_____ dressed, and then we [4]_____ home at about 8:30 a.m. Leon goes to school, and I'm an office worker. I [5]_____ work at 9:00 a.m.
I [6]_____ work at 3:00 p.m. and go to Leon's school. We [7]_____ grocery shopping and [8]_____ home at about 4:00 in the afternoon. In the evening, Leon [9]_____ his homework and I make dinner. After dinner, Leon [10]_____ to bed at 8:00 p.m. and I [11]_____ housework and [12]_____ to the radio. I go to bed at 11:00 p.m. … and the next day, we do it all again!

◀ Go back to page 32

VOCABULARY PRACTICE

4B Transportation

1 ▶ 4.6 Listen and repeat.

1 by bike

2 by boat

3 by bus

4 by car

5 by ferry

6 by motorcycle

7 by plane

8 by taxi

9 by train

10 by truck

11 on foot

12 on the subway/Underground/metro

Look! Different cities have different names for their underground trains.
In New York, I go on the **subway**.   In London, I go on the **underground**.   In Sydney, I go on the **metro**.

2 Match the types of transportation in the box with the pictures.

| truck | taxi | subway | ferry | train | plane | boat | motorcycle |

3 Complete the sentences with the correct types of transportation and *by* or *on*.

1 I go _____ 🚲 to the train station. Then I go _____ 🚆 downtown. After that, I go _____ 🚶 to the office.

2 Lucia goes _____ 🚕 to the airport. Then she goes _____ ✈ to New York. After that, she goes downtown _____ 🚇.

3 We go _____ 🚗 to Boston, but my brother goes _____ 🏍. Then we all go _____ 🚢 to Provincetown.

◀ Go back to page 34

115

VOCABULARY PRACTICE

3B Days and times of day

1 ▶ 3.7 Listen and repeat.

12 morning 13 afternoon 14 evening 15 night

Look! We use the preposition *on* with days of the week and *the weekend*, *in* with *the morning*, *the afternoon*, and *the evening*, and *at* with *night*.
I eat fish on Friday.
I go grocery shopping on the weekend.
I have breakfast in the morning.
I drink milk at night.

We also say *on* + day and time of day:
on Wednesday morning, on Friday afternoon, etc.

2 Chose the correct words to complete the sentences and questions.

1 My birthday's *on / in / at* Sunday.
2 I have dinner *on / in / at* the evening.
3 We don't drink coffee at *afternoon / evening / night*.
4 I have lunch with Emma on *the afternoon / Friday / the morning*.
5 Is your English class *on / in / at* Thursday evening?
6 They have breakfast at 9:00 in *the weekend / Wednesday / the morning*.
7 Is Marcus on vacation *on / in / at* Thursday?
8 They don't have classes *on / in / at* Wednesday afternoons.
9 What do you eat on the *afternoon / weekend / the night*?
10 On Sunday, I have chicken for lunch *on / in / at* the afternoon.

◀ Go back to page 26

4C Adjectives (2)

1 ▶ 4.7 Listen and repeat.

1 cold 2 hot 3 clean 4 dirty 5 fast 6 slow 7 friendly 8 unfriendly

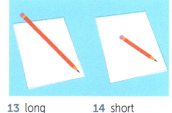

9 nice 10 horrible 11 large 12 small 13 long 14 short 15 noisy 16 quiet

2 Complete the text with the adjectives in the box.

| noisy | cold | quiet | hot | short | friendly | dirty | large |

Hi, I'm Matt. I'm a student in Seattle, Washington. I always get up at 8:30 and I have a ¹_____ tea for breakfast. Then, I go to school on foot. It's sometimes ²_____ in the mornings, but that's OK – it's only a ³_____ walk.

I live in a ⁴_____ house with eight students. They're really ⁵_____ . We always make dinner together, and sometimes there are a lot of ⁶_____ dishes when we finish! My roommates play music, and the house is sometimes ⁷_____ , so I usually work in the library – it's always ⁸_____ there.

◀ Go back to page 36

VOCABULARY PRACTICE

5A Common verbs (2)

1 ▶ 5.1 Listen and repeat.

1 **arrive** at the airport

2 **call** my mother

3 **take care of** my daughter

4 **cook** fish

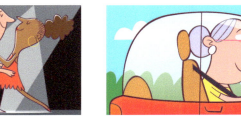
5 **dance** salsa

6 **drive** a car

7 **give** a gift

8 **help** my grandmother

9 **meet** friends

10 **play** soccer

11 **play** the piano

12 **sing**

13 **speak** Italian

14 **swim** in the ocean

15 **travel** by bus

2 Complete the sentences with the correct form of the verbs in the box.

cook meet give arrive help drive speak play (x2) travel sing call take care of

1 Simon _____ Portuguese.
2 I _____ dinner on the weekend.
3 Sharon often _____ basketball.
4 My father _____ a bus.
5 I always _____ my son with his homework.
6 We usually _____ by train.
7 I sometimes _____ my friend's dog.
8 We _____ in Lima at 9:15 a.m.
9 I always _____ Lucy for a coffee after work.
10 You never _____ me flowers.
11 Jo likes music. She _____ and _____ the guitar.
12 My parents live in India, so I _____ them on Skype.

◀ Go back to page 42

117

VOCABULARY PRACTICE

5B Electronic devices

1 ▶ 5.8 Listen and repeat.

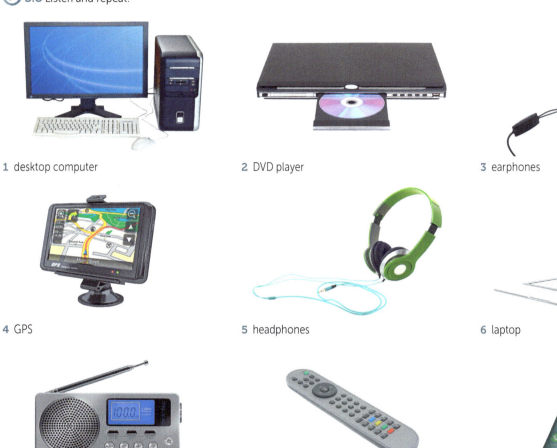

1 desktop computer
2 DVD player
3 earphones
4 GPS
5 headphones
6 laptop
7 radio
8 remote control
9 smartphone
10 smart speaker
11 tablet
12 TV (television)

2 Cross out the word which is incorrect in each sentence.

1 A Listen to this song on my phone – it's great!
   B Hold on – I need some *earphones / remote control / headphones*.
2 A Can I check my e-mail?
   B Yes. You can use my *radio / tablet / smartphone*.
3 A My friend lives on Bridge Street, but I don't know where that is.
   B It's OK. I have a *smartphone / GPS / headphones*. We can use that.
4 A Do you want to watch a movie tonight?
   B We can't. I don't have a *remote control / TV / DVD player*.
5 A I work at home. I have a *laptop / TV / desktop computer* and that's all I need.
   B At home? What a nice job!
6 A It's quiet. Why don't we listen to some music?
   B OK ... here's my *radio / GPS / smart speaker*.
7 A The news is on at 12:00.
   B OK, the *DVD player / TV / radio* is over there.
8 A Do you have a TV?
   B No, I don't. I watch TV shows on my *laptop / radio / smartphone*.

118   ◀ Go back to page 44

VOCABULARY PRACTICE

5C Activities

1 ▶ 5.13 Listen and repeat.

1 bike riding

2 cleaning

3 cooking

4 dancing

5 going out

6 hiking

7 listening to music

8 meeting friends

9 reading

10 running

11 shopping

12 sleeping

13 swimming

14 watching TV/movies

Look! We can use activities that end in *-ing* or nouns with the verbs *like*, *love*, and *hate*.
I like shopping.   I love clothes!
I don't like bike riding.   I hate bikes.

2 Match the activities in the box with pictures 1–8.

| swimming   reading   running   cooking   bike riding   cleaning   shopping   sleeping |

1 _____

2 _____

3 _____

4 _____

5 _____

6 _____

7 _____

8 _____

◀ Go back to page 46

VOCABULARY PRACTICE

6A Places in town

1 ▶ 6.1 Listen and repeat.

 1 bank
 2 bus stop
 3 café
 4 club
 5 hospital
 6 hotel
 7 movie theater
 8 museum
 9 park
 10 police station
 11 post office
 12 restaurant
 13 school
 14 shopping mall
 15 grocery store
 16 train station

Look!

 a town
 a city

A town is small or medium-sized.
A city is big.

2 Match the places in the box with jobs 1–5.

| hospital   police station   school |
| restaurant   shopping mall |

1 waiter _____
2 police officer _____
3 salesclerk _____
4 teacher _____
5 doctor _____

3 Complete the sentences with the places in the box.

| bank   club   train station   park   post office   grocery store |
| bus stop   café   movie theater   museum |

1 You can send a letter at a _____ .
2 You can catch a train at a _____ .
3 You wait for a bus at a _____ .
4 You drink tea or coffee at a _____ .
5 You can dance at a _____ .
6 You watch a movie at a _____ .
7 You see interesting things at a _____ .
8 You get money at a _____ .
9 You walk, play games, or relax in a _____ .
10 You can buy food and drinks at a _____ .

◀ Go back to page 50

VOCABULARY PRACTICE

6B Parts of the body

1 ▶ 6.7 Listen and repeat.

Look! The plural of *tooth* is *teeth*. The plural of *foot* is *feet*.

1 hair
2 head
3 ear
4 face
5 eye
6 nose
7 tooth (teeth)
8 mouth
9 body
10 arm
11 hand
12 leg
13 knee
14 foot (feet)

2 Put the parts of the body in the box in the correct columns.

| arms   body   ears   face   feet   hands   head   knees   legs   mouth   nose   teeth |

I have one …	I have two …	I have more than two …

◀ Go back to page 52

121

VOCABULARY PRACTICE

6C Rooms and furniture

1 ▶ 6.8 Listen and repeat.

2 Complete the sentences with the rooms and furniture in the box.

| refrigerator | bathtub | table | sofa | desk | window | bedroom | stove | closet | shelves |

1 Let's have dinner in the living room. We can sit on the _____ and watch a movie.
2 Shona has a big walk-in _____ for all her clothes.
3 My favorite room is my _____ . I sleep there, and it's very quiet.
4 After we make dinner, the _____ is very hot.
5 My bathroom is small, so I take a shower, but I don't have a _____ .
6 Angie needs a lot of _____ because she has hundreds of books!
7 It's hot in here. Can you open the _____ ?
8 Please put the milk and orange juice in the _____ .
9 I have a _____ in my bedroom where I do homework and use my laptop.
10 Dinner's ready. The food's on the _____ !

◀ Go back to page 54

VOCABULARY PRACTICE

7A Celebrities

1 ▶ 7.1 Listen and repeat.

 1 artist
 2 athlete
 3 dancer
 4 DJ

 5 fashion model
 6 journalist
 7 king
 8 movie director

 9 musician
 10 photographer
 11 politician
 12 queen

 13 racing driver
 14 soccer player
 15 tennis player
 16 writer

2 Look at the pictures and complete the sentences with the words in the box.

| fashion model | writer | queen | musician | tennis player | dancer | king | movie director | artist | soccer player | politician | athlete |

 1 Shelly-Ann Fraser-Pryce is a Jamaican _____ .
 2 Gisele Bündchen is a Brazilian _____ .
 3 Emmanuel Macron is a French _____ .
 4 Isabel Allende is a Chilean _____ .
 5 Thomas Müller is a German _____ .
 6 Margrethe II is the _____ of Denmark.

 7 Salvador Dalí was a Spanish _____ .
 8 Beyoncé is an American _____ .
 9 Sofia Coppola is an American _____ .
 10 Venus Williams is an American _____ .
 11 Felipe VI is the _____ of Spain.
 12 Rudolf Nureyev was a Russian _____ .

◀ Go back to page 60

123

VOCABULARY PRACTICE

7B Months and ordinals

1 ▶ 7.5 Listen and repeat.

1 January	2 February	3 March	4 April
5 May	6 June	7 July	8 August
9 September	10 October	11 November	12 December

2 ▶ 7.6 Listen and repeat.

1st	first	7th	seventh	13th	thirteenth	19th	nineteenth
2nd	second	8th	eighth	14th	fourteenth	20th	twentieth
3rd	third	9th	ninth	15th	fifteenth	21st	twenty-first
4th	fourth	10th	tenth	16th	sixteenth	22nd	twenty-second
5th	fifth	11th	eleventh	17th	seventeenth	30th	thirtieth
6th	sixth	12th	twelfth	18th	eighteenth	31st	thirty-first

> **Look!** In American English, the ordinal comes after the month.
>
> *February 2 = February second*
> *June 16 = June sixteenth*

3 Look at the dates in parentheses and complete the sentences with the words.

1 Valentine's Day is _____ _____ . (2/14)
2 Independence Day in the U.S. is _____ _____ . (7/4)
3 New Year's Day is _____ _____ . (1/1)
4 Veterans Day is _____ _____ . (11/11)
5 My birthday is _____ _____ . (7/25)
6 Cinco de Mayo is _____ _____ . (5/5)

◀ Go back to page 62

7C Time expressions

1 ▶ 7.14 Listen and repeat.

1	last	last night, last week, last year
2	ago	two days ago, three weeks ago, four years ago
3	yesterday	yesterday morning, yesterday afternoon, yesterday evening
4	times	at 9:00, at 11:30, at midnight
5	days	on Monday, on Tuesdays, on the weekend
6	dates	on January 1, on April 24, on December 11
7	years	in 1985, in 2001, in 2018
8	decades	in the 1960s, in the 1990s, in the 2010s

2 Complete the sentences with the words in the box.

> on (x2)   in   ago   last (x2)   yesterday   at

1 I studied English _____ morning. Then I watched TV.
2 We enjoyed your party _____ night. It was great!
3 Samantha meets her friends _____ 6:30 after work.
4 I lived in Madrid _____ the 1980s. It was an interesting time.
5 My brother traveled to Europe _____ year.
6 I started my new job _____ November 4.
7 My grandmother was a teacher 50 years _____ .
8 I usually finish work early _____ Fridays.

◀ Go back to page 65

VOCABULARY PRACTICE

8A Travel verbs

1 ▶ 8.1 Listen and repeat.

1 **book** a flight

2 **fly**

3 **get in** a taxi

4 **get lost**

5 **get off** a bus

6 **get on** a train

7 **get out of** a taxi

8 **miss** the bus

9 **ride** a bike

10 **sail**

11 **take** the subway

12 **walk**

2 Check (✓) the verbs we can use with each type of transportation.

	a taxi	a bike	a boat	a plane	a bus	a train
ride						
take						
miss						
get in / out of						
get on / off						
sail						

3 Choose the correct words to complete the sentences.

1 Anne needs to *walk / book* a ticket for her trip to Los Angeles.
2 This is our bus stop. Quick, *get off / get out* now!
3 Let's *walk / get out* home. It's a nice warm evening.
4 Juan decided to *sail / fly* to Spain because he hates planes.
5 When the train arrived, a lot of people tried to *get lost / get on*.
6 There are no trains. We need to *ride / take* a taxi home.
7 They *missed / booked* their bus, so they arrived really late.
8 I can drive you home if you want. *Get in / Get out*!
9 Stuart *drives / rides* a motorcycle because it's fast.
10 You can *take / fly* the number 35 bus downtown.

◀ Go back to page 68

VOCABULARY PRACTICE

8B Weather and seasons

1 ▶ 8.6 Listen and repeat.

1 hot
2 warm
3 cold
4 cloudy
5 sunny
6 wet
7 dry
8 windy
9 foggy
10 rain
11 snow
12 spring
13 summer
14 fall
15 winter

Look! *rain* and *snow* are verbs. To talk about the weather now, we say *It's raining/It's snowing*. To talk about the weather in general, we say *It rains/It snows*.

2 Look at the weather map and complete the sentences.

1 It's _____ in Moscow.
2 It's _____ in Bogotá.
3 It's _____ in Rio de Janeiro.
4 It's _____ in New York.
5 It's _____ in Tokyo.
6 It's _____ in Hong Kong.
7 It's _____ in Anchorage.
8 It's _____ in Johannesburg.
9 It's _____ in Melbourne.

◀ Go back to page 70

VOCABULARY PRACTICE

8C Nature

1 ▶ 8.7 Listen and repeat.

1 beach
2 cloud
3 field
4 flower
5 forest
6 grass
7 mountain
8 ocean
9 river
10 sky
11 sun
12 tree

2 Choose the correct words to complete the sentences.
   1 Kilimanjaro is a *beach / mountain* in Tanzania.
   2 The Nile is a *river / field* in Africa.
   3 The Amazon is a *forest / mountain* in South America.
   4 The rose is a *cloud / flower* that can be different colors.
   5 Bermuda is in the Atlantic *Ocean / River*.
   6 Copacabana is a *beach / forest* in Brazil.
   7 Apples are a fruit that come from a *grass / tree*.
   8 The temperature of the *sun / sky* is 15 million °C.
   9 Cumulus, cirrus, and stratus are *clouds / trees*.
   10 Animals like horses and rabbits eat *trees / grass*.

◀ Go back to page 72

127

VOCABULARY PRACTICE

9A Clothes

1 ▶ 9.1 Listen and repeat.

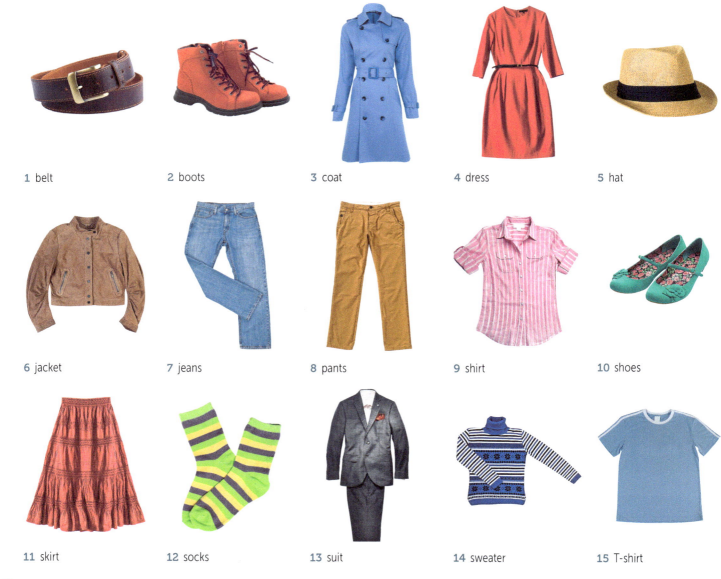

1 belt
2 boots
3 coat
4 dress
5 hat
6 jacket
7 jeans
8 pants
9 shirt
10 shoes
11 skirt
12 socks
13 suit
14 sweater
15 T-shirt

2 Write the clothes from exercise 1 in the correct places.

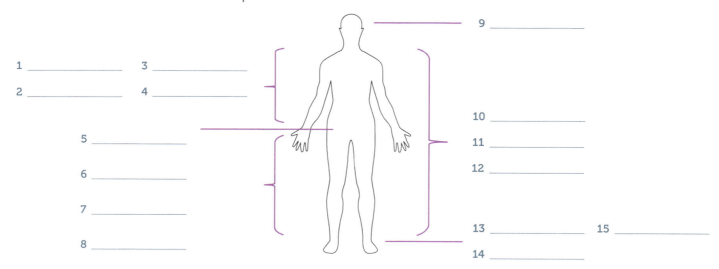

128

◀ Go back to page 78

VOCABULARY PRACTICE

9B Feelings

1 ▶ 9.6 Listen and repeat.

 1 angry
 2 bored
 3 calm
 4 excited
 5 happy
 6 hungry
 7 sad
 8 scared
 9 surprised
 10 thirsty
 11 tired
 12 worried

2 Choose the correct adjective to complete the sentences.

1 Can I have a glass of water? I'm really *hungry / thirsty*.
2 He's *surprised / worried* about money because he doesn't have a job.
3 I'm *bored / scared*. This movie's not very interesting.
4 It's Louisa's birthday tomorrow – she's very *excited / tired*.
5 I like yoga because it makes me feel *calm / sad*.
6 Are you *angry / hungry*? Do you want a sandwich?
7 You're very *scared / tired*. Why don't you go to bed?
8 Tim is *angry / hungry* with me because I broke his computer.
9 I was *bored / surprised* that John ran a marathon because he doesn't like sports.
10 Suzie doesn't like horror movies. They make her feel *scared / surprised*.

3 Match the feelings in the box with the messages.

tired   sad   worried   angry   surprised

1 **Julia** I get my grades today! 😬
2 **Ying-Li** I arrived in Chicago today after a 10-hour flight. 😴
3 **Saanvi** I won the science competition. I can't believe it! 😱
4 **Dave** All my friends are in Hawaii on vacation. I'm at work. 😣
5 **Hans** I lost my wallet on the train today … and I was late for work. 😠

◀ Go back to page 80

129

VOCABULARY PRACTICE

9C Shopping

1 ▶ 9.12 Listen and repeat.

1 buy a car

2 go shopping

3 pay by credit card

4 pay with cash

5 sell ice cream

6 shop online

7 spend money

8 try on clothes

9 department store

10 local stores

11 market

12 shopping mall

2 Match the sentence parts to make full sentences.

1 I always pay by
2 We usually spend
3 Can I try on
4 I never shop
5 Jorge sells
6 Malika wants to buy
7 You can only pay with
8 We need to go

a these jeans, please?
b a new laptop.
c fish in the market.
d grocery shopping.
e $100 every weekend.
f credit card. It's easy!
g cash in this store.
h online. I like real stores.

3 Choose the correct words to complete the sentences.

1 I don't *go / buy* shopping on Saturdays. There are lots of people.
2 My brother works for a technology company. He *spends / sells* computers.
3 Sharon lives in a small town. There are only three or four *department stores / local stores*.
4 Carla *spends / buys* all her money on clothes.
5 When we go on vacation, we usually pay *with / by* credit card.
6 The *shopping mall / market* near us has a movie theater and lots of restaurants.
7 I always *try / shop* on clothes before I buy them.
8 My cell phone is broken. I need to *buy / pay* a new one.

130   ◀ Go back to page 82

VOCABULARY PRACTICE

10A Free-time activities

1 ▶ 10.1 Listen and repeat.

1 go to a concert

2 go to a festival

3 go to the beach

4 have a barbecue

5 have a good time

6 have a party

7 stay at a hotel

8 stay home

9 stay in a tent

10 visit a museum

11 visit an art gallery

12 visit family/friends

13 watch a movie

14 watch a soccer game

15 watch a video

2 Match the activities in the box with the people.

> visit family   go to the beach   have a barbecue   watch a movie
> have a party   stay home   visit a museum   stay in a tent

1 Erica likes hot weather and swimming. She has two new books to read. _____
2 It's a beautiful sunny day. Paul is hungry, and he has some meat and fish. _____
3 It's Lucia's birthday tomorrow, and she wants to celebrate with her friends. _____
4 The weather's not good, and Samuel has an exam next week. _____
5 Marek and Kasia are in Charleston for the weekend. They're interested in history. _____
6 Sonia loves nature. She wants to go on vacation, but she doesn't want to spend a lot of money. _____
7 Cristian is going to San Francisco. His family lives there. _____
8 Natalia is at home tonight. She bought a new 40-inch TV last week. _____

◀ Go back to page 86

VOCABULARY PRACTICE

10B Types of music and movies

1 ▶ 10.9 Listen and repeat.

1 classical music

2 electronic music

3 hip-hop music

4 jazz music

5 pop music

6 rock music

7 an action movie

8 a comedy

9 a drama

10 a horror movie

11 a romance

12 a science-fiction movie

2 Look at the pictures and write the types of music and movies.

1 _____

2 _____

3 _____

4 _____

5 _____

6 _____

◀ Go back to page 88

VOCABULARY PRACTICE

10C Sports and games

1 ▶ 10.10 Listen and repeat.

1 do gymnastics

2 do karate

3 do pilates

4 do yoga

5 go bike riding

6 go hiking

7 go rock climbing

8 go running

9 go skiing

10 go swimming

11 play baseball

12 play basketball

13 play chess

14 play hockey

15 play soccer

16 play tennis

17 play videogames

18 play volleyball

> **Look!**
> We use *play* with sports that use a ball and with games.
> *I play golf.*
> We use *go* with activities that end in *-ing*.
> *I go sailing.*
> We use *do* with individual activities and sports that don't use a ball.
> *I do judo.*

2 Complete the sentences with the correct form of *go*, *play*, or *do*.

1 He usually _____ tennis on the weekend.
2 It's a beautiful sunny day. Why don't we _____ hiking?
3 They _____ gymnastics every Monday after school.
4 Do you want to _____ chess later?
5 Did you _____ bike riding last weekend?
6 She often _____ pilates to relax.
7 I _____ skiing with my parents every winter.
8 Do your children _____ a lot of videogames?

◀ Go back to page 90

133

COMMUNICATION PRACTICE

Hello Student A

1 Look at the labels. Ask Student B for the name of the city.
   A *What's LHR?*
   B *I think it's London.*
   A *How do you spell that?*
   B *L-O-N-D-O-N.*

2 Listen to Student B's airport codes. Tell him/her the correct city for the letters.

   | New Delhi   Cape Town   Barcelona   New York   Amsterdam |

1. LHR _____
2. MEX _____
3. IST _____
4. LAX _____
5. HGK _____

1A Student A

1 You are Mehmet. Answer Student B's questions with the information.
   B *What's your name?*
   A *I'm Mehmet Guliyev.*
   B *How do you spell that?*
   A *M-E-H-M-E-T ...*

Name:	Mehmet Guliyev
Nationality:	Turkish
Phone:	90 312 213 2965

2 Ask Student B the questions and write down his/her answers.
   1 What's your name?
   _____
   2 Where are you from?
   _____
   3 What's your phone number?
   _____

1C Student A

1 Ask Student B questions about the Antarctic Zebras to complete the information.

   Where are they from?   How old is Bev?   What is her job?

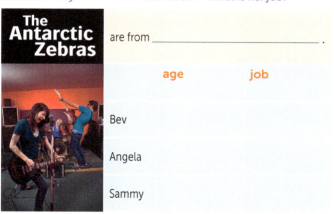

are from _____ .

	age	job
Bev		
Angela		
Sammy		

2 Now look at the information about the Rocking Stones. Answer Student B's questions.

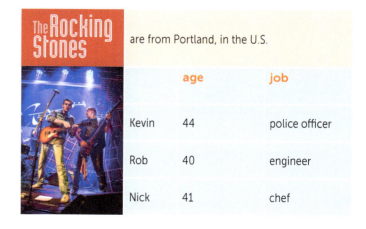

are from Portland, in the U.S.

	age	job
Kevin	44	police officer
Rob	40	engineer
Nick	41	chef

COMMUNICATION PRACTICE

2A Students A and B

1 Look at the picture. In pairs, ask about the objects.
   What's this/that?   What are these/those?

2 Now, turn to page 143 and check your ideas.

2C Student A

Ask and answer questions with Student B to complete David and Victoria Beckham's family tree.

A *What's David's mother's name?*
B *Her name is …*

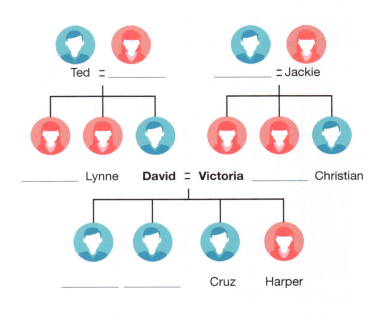

2D Student A

1 Ask Student B the questions and write down the answers. Remember to be polite.

   A *Excuse me, what time's the next train to Boston, please?*
   B *It's at eleven forty-five.*
   A *Thanks.*
   1 What time's the next train to Boston? _____
   2 What's Lucy's phone number? _____
   3 Where's the teacher from? _____
   4 How old are you? _____
   5 What's the name of the café? _____

2 Answer Student B's questions with the answers in the box.

   | He's 28.   She's from Mexico.   You're in Room 48. |
   | It's F-O-S-T-E-R.   It's at 6:40. |

135

COMMUNICATION PRACTICE

3A Student A

1 Ask Student B questions to complete the information.

A *What do you have for breakfast?*
B *For breakfast, I eat ...*

breakfast	lunch	dinner

2 Look at the information. Answer Student B's questions about your breakfast, lunch, and dinner.

3C Student A

1 Ask Student B questions about Maggie to complete the information in the chart.

A *Does Maggie live in a city?*
B *Yes, she does. She lives in Sacramento.*

	Maggie	Antonio
work in an office?		✗ (he / work / in a school)
live in a city?		✓
have children?		✓ (he / have / two daughters)
watch TV in the morning?		✗ (he / work)
use public transportation every day?		✓
go to the gym after work?		✗ (he / make / dinner)
study in the evening?		✗ (he / watch / TV)
play sports on the weekend?		✓

2 Look at the information about Antonio. Answer Student B's questions and give extra information when you can.

B *Does Antonio work in an office?*   A *No, he doesn't. He works at a school.*

4A Student A

1 Write sentences in the simple present with the frequency adverbs in parentheses. Then read them to Student B.

1 Leila / watch / movies on her phone. (sometimes)
_____

2 Dean / wake up / before 6:00 a.m. (often)
_____

3 Paulo / read / in bed. (usually)
_____

4 Marta / be / late for work. (never)
_____

5 Shaun / cook / dinner for his family. (always)
_____

2 Listen to Student B. Match the names in the box with the people.

Danny   Nina   Eric   Claire   Tom

1 _____ 2 _____ 3 _____ 4 _____ 5 _____

I usually finish work after 7:00 p.m.   *I'm often at the library at night.*   *I always drink tea for breakfast.*   *I never take a bath in the morning.*   *I sometimes go to the gym on Saturdays.*

COMMUNICATION PRACTICE

4C Student A

1 Ask Student B questions about Ella. Write his/her answers.

A *Where does Ella live?*   B *She lives in Philadelphia.*

Ella

Questions

Where / live?
What / do?
Where / work?
What time / get up?
What time / finish work?
Why / like her job?
How / relax in the evening?
What / do on the weekend?

2 Read Zain's profile. Listen to Student B and answer his/her questions.

Zain

Hi, I'm Zain. I live in Los Angeles. I'm a waiter at a big hotel in Hollywood. I get up at 8:00 a.m., and before work I usually go to the gym. I start work at 11:00, and I finish at 9:00 p.m. I like my job because I meet interesting people. To relax in the evening, I play the guitar. I usually work on the weekend.

4D Student A

1 You are a customer. Ask Student B for the things on your shopping list. Then ask how much each thing is. Remember to be polite.

A *Good morning. Can I have a cheese sandwich, please?*
B *Here you are.*
A *Thank you. How much is it?*
B *$1.99. Anything else?*

Shopping list
1 cheese sandwich
6 eggs
some orange juice
some coffee
some pasta
Total price = ?

2 You are a salesclerk. Serve Student B. Remember to be polite.

```
2x bottles water     $1.60
fish                 $5.80
1x pizza (4 cheese)  $3.99
1 box salad          $1.50
1 chocolate cake     $3.85
Total                $16.74
```

5A Student A

1 Look at the chart. Ask questions with *can* to guess which person Student B has.

A *Can she drive?*
B *Yes, she can.*

2 Answer Student B's questions about Mark. You can only say *Yes, he can* or *No, he can't.*

	Annie	Mona	Sara	Lucy	Hana	Kim
Can / drive?	✗	✓	✓	✓	✓	✓
Can / speak Spanish?	✗	✓	✓	✗	✓	✗
Can / play the guitar?	✓	✗	✓	✗	✓	✗
Can / cook Chinese food?	✓	✓	✗	✓	✗	✗
Can / dance salsa?	✗	✗	✓	✗	✗	✓

MARK

He can swim well and write computer programs.
He can't take care of children, play the piano, or speak French.

COMMUNICATION PRACTICE

5C Student A

1 Look at the profiles for a website called *New Friends*. Ask and answer questions with Student B to complete the information.

A *What does Daniela think about cooking?* B *She likes it.*

☺☺ = love, ☺ = like, ☹ = not like, ☹☹ = hate

Daniela
- cooking
- cats and dogs
- early mornings

Bill
- hiking
- housework
- books

Monica
- going out
- bike riding
- movies

Miguel
- ☹ cleaning
- ☺☺ reading
- ☹☹ sports

Claudio
- ☺ swimming
- ☺☺ watching movies
- ☹ dancing

Lucy
- ☺ sleeping
- ☺ animals
- ☺☺ food and drink

2 Look at the profiles again. Find the best new friend for each person.

6A Student A

Look at the picture. Ask and answer questions with Student B to find six differences.

A *Are there any hotels?*
B *Yes, there are. There are two hotels.*
A *In my picture, there's one hotel.*
B *Is there a movie theater?*

6C Student A

1 Describe your picture to Student B. He/She will draw it.

A *There's a bed. Next to the bed, there's a small table.*

2 Listen to Student B and draw the room.

B *There's a sofa in front of the window.*

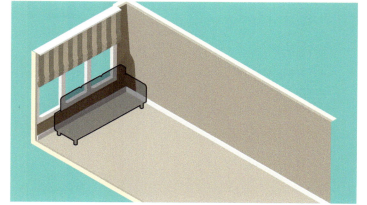

138

COMMUNICATION PRACTICE

6D Student A

1 Ask Student B for directions to the places in the box. Listen and mark on the map where they are. Check the information if you need to.

| post office   bank   Internet café |

A *Excuse me, is there a post office near here?*
B *Yes, there is. You go down Market Street …*
A *Could you repeat that, please?*

2 Listen to Student B. Look at the map and give directions.

7A Student A

1 Ask Student B questions with *was* to match the famous people with their jobs and where they were from.

A *Was Federico Fellini an artist?*
B *No, he wasn't.*

1 Federico Fellini   writer   South Africa
2 Janis Joplin   politician   the U.S.
3 Nelson Mandela   movie director   Colombia
4 Greta Garbo   artist   Japan
5 Katsushika Hokusai   singer   Italy
6 Gabriel García Márquez actor   Sweden

2 Answer Student B's questions about the famous people. You can only say *Yes, he/she was* or *No, he/she wasn't*.

1 Frida Kahlo was an artist from Mexico.
2 Johan Cruyff was a soccer player from the Netherlands.
3 Celia Cruz was a singer from Cuba.
4 Jane Austen was a writer from the UK.
5 Paco de Lucía was a musician from Spain.
6 Jawaharlal Nehru was a politician from India.

7C Student A

1 Ask Student B questions. Find one incorrect piece of information for each person.

A *Did Luke visit his grandparents last week?*
B *No, he didn't. He visited his grandparents last month.*

1 Luke / visit / his grandparents / last ~~week~~   month
2 Kenny / travel / to Brazil / three years ago
3 Clara / play / volleyball / yesterday
4 Debbie / cook / noodles / last night
5 Steve / work / as a teacher / in the 1980s
6 Amelia / watch / a TV show / yesterday morning

2 Listen to Student B's questions. Correct the information.

1 Zoe stayed at a hotel downtown last year.
2 Jim studied Spanish in college in the 1990s.
3 Antonia walked 18 miles yesterday.
4 Leandro watched a soccer game three days ago.
5 Rachel started a new job in London last month.
6 Tom finished work one hour ago.

7A London's famous houses: answers

1 Mahatma Gandhi

2 Bob Marley

3 Agatha Christie

4 Vincent van Gogh

139

COMMUNICATION PRACTICE

8A Student A

1 Ask Student B questions to find out what Lola did yesterday.

A *Where did Lola go?*
B *She went to her dad's birthday party.*

2 Read the information and answer Student B's questions about what Mateo did yesterday.

Lola

Where / go?
What time / leave / the house?
she / take / the bus?
What / wear?
What / buy / for her dad?
she / have / a good time?
Where / sleep / last night?

Mateo

He / go / Rome
He / fly
He / take / taxi to the airport
His flight / leave at 11:00 a.m.
He / go / with friends
He / sleep / on a plane for 20 minutes
He / have / a good trip

8C Student A

1 Look at the picture for one minute. Then close your book and answer Student B's questions.

2 Give Student B one minute to look at his/her picture. Ask him/her questions with *Was/Were there a/an/any ...?* and the words in the box. If he/she answers *Yes, there were*, ask *How many were there?*

| boats | hospital | cars | flowers |
| birds | stores | beach | river |

A *Were there any boats?*   B *Yes, there were.*
A *How many were there?*   B *There was one boat.*

8D Student A

1 Read the situation in the box, and then look at the flowchart. You are the receptionist. Student B calls you. Have the conversation.

A *Hello, Green Lane Medical Center. Jorge speaking. How can I help you?*
B *Hello, my name's Anna Lopez. I'd like to see the doctor.*

> You work at the Green Lane Medical Center. Answer the phone. Ask the person what the problem is.

Receptionist

- Answer the phone. Give the name of the medical center/sports center and your name.
- Ask more detailed questions.
- Ask for the caller's contact details.
- Finish the call.

Patient/Customer

- Introduce yourself and say why you are calling.
- Answer.
- Answer.

2 Read the situation in the box, and then look at the flowchart again. You are the customer. Call Student B and have the conversation.

> You want to join a sports center. You're interested in swimming and tennis.
> Your phone number is 555-1212.

COMMUNICATION PRACTICE

9C Student A

Ask and answer the question *How often do/does ...?* with Student B to complete the chart.

A *How often do Jon and Andy go to the movies?*
B *They go to the movies three or four times a year.*

Laura	have dinner in a restaurant	twice a month
Jon and Andy	go to the movies	
Carlota	shop online	once or twice a week
Ahmed	ride a motorcycle	
Hope and Sara	check their e-mails	four or five times a day
Igor	read a new book	
Luisa and Raul	go swimming	every week
Yannis	go on vacation	

10A Student A

Look at your schedule. Try to find a time when you can meet Student B. Ask and answer the question *What are you doing on ...?* for the different days.

A *What are you doing on Monday morning?*
B *I'm going to the gym. What about Monday afternoon?*

	Monday	Tuesday	Wednesday	Thursday	Friday
Morning			travel to the city		
Afternoon	see doctor	have lunch with parents	visit National Museum		
Evening	watch movie at movie theater		stay with friends		have dinner with Carl

10C Student A

Ask Student B questions about his/her hobby in the correct tense. Write down his/her answers. Then guess what the hobby is.

A *How often do you do your hobby?*
B *I do it twice a week.*

Student B's hobby

Your hobby: rock climbing

1 How often / you / do / your hobby?
2 When / you / start?
3 it / be / expensive?
4 it / be / dangerous?
5 you / play / it in a team?
6 How many people / be there / in your team?
7 Where / you / do / your hobby?
8 you / do / your hobby next weekend?

Every weekend.
When I was 14.
No, it's not.
It can be.
No, but I always go with another person.
–
Sometimes at a sports center, sometimes in the mountains.
Yes, I'm driving to the beach on Friday night.

141

COMMUNICATION PRACTICE

Hello Student B

1 Listen to Student A's airport codes. Tell him/her the correct city for the letters.

> Hong Kong   Los Angeles   Mexico City   London   Istanbul

A *What's LHR?*
B *I think it's London.*
A *How do you spell that?*
B *L-O-N-D-O-N.*

2 Look at the labels. Ask Student A for the name of the city.

1 _____ 2 _____ 3 _____

4 _____ 5 _____

1A Student B

1 Ask Student A the questions and write down his/her answers.

1 What's your name?
   _____
2 Where are you from?
   _____
3 What's your phone number?
   _____

2 You are Saori. Answer Student A's questions with the information.

A *What's your name?*
B *I'm Saori Arakawa.*
A *How do you spell that?*
B *S-A-O-R-I ...*

Name:	Saori Arakawa
Nationality:	Japanese
Phone:	81 90 1790 1357

1C Student B

1 Look at the information about the Antarctic Zebras. Answer Student A's questions.

are from Chicago, in the U.S.

	age	job
Bev	19	student
Angela	24	IT worker
Sammy	25	tour guide

2 Now ask Student A questions about the Rocking Stones to complete the information.

Where are they from?   *How old is Kevin?*   *What is his job?*

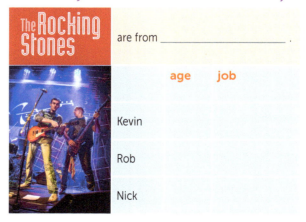

are from _____.

	age	job
Kevin		
Rob		
Nick		

COMMUNICATION PRACTICE

2A Students A and B

Look at the picture. In pairs, discuss if you were right or wrong.

A *This is a pen.*
B *You're right.*

2C Student B

Ask and answer questions with Student A to complete David and Victoria Beckham's family tree.

B *What's Victoria's mother's name?*
A *Her name is ....*

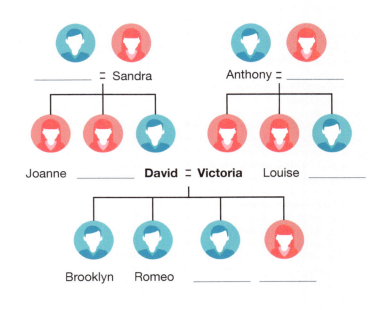

2D Student B

1 Answer Student A's questions with the answers in the box.

I'm 39.   It's 07700 900638.   The Oak Tree Café.
It's at 11:45.   He's from Canada.

2 Ask Student A the questions and write down the answers. Remember to be polite.

B *Excuse me, what time's the flight to Los Angeles, please?*
A *It's at six forty.*
B *Thanks.*

1 What time's the flight to Los Angeles? _____
2 How old is the teacher? _____
3 Where's María from? _____
4 What room am I in? _____
5 How do you spell your last name? _____

143

COMMUNICATION PRACTICE

3A Student B

1. Look at the information. Answer Student A's questions about your breakfast, lunch, and dinner.

2. Ask Student A questions to complete the information.
   B *What do you have for breakfast?*
   A *For breakfast, I eat …*

breakfast	lunch	dinner

3C Student B

1. Look at the information about Maggie. Answer Student A's questions and give extra information when you can.

   A *Does Maggie live in a city?*
   B *Yes, she does. She lives in Sacramento.*

	Maggie	Antonio
work in an office?	✓	
live in a city?	✓ (she / live / in Sacramento)	
have children?	✗ (she / have / two cats)	
watch TV in the morning?	✗	
use public transportation every day?	✗ (she / walk / to work)	
go to the gym after work?	✓	
study in the evening?	✓ (she / study / English)	
play sports on weekends?	✗ (she / make / cakes)	

2. Ask Student A questions about Antonio to complete the information in the chart.
   B *Does Antonio work in an office?*   A *No, he doesn't. He works at a school.*

4A Student B

1. Listen to Student A. Match the names in the box with the people.

   | Marta Shaun Leila Dean Paulo |

   1 _____   2 _____   3 _____   4 _____   5 _____

   I often wake up before 6:00 a.m. *I'm never late for work.* *I usually read in bed.* *I sometimes watch movies on my phone.* *I always cook dinner for my family.*

2. Write sentences in the simple present with the frequency adverbs in parentheses. Then read them to Student A.

   1 Claire / drink / tea for breakfast. (always)
   _____
   2 Tom / go / to the gym on Saturdays. (sometimes)
   _____
   3 Eric / take / a bath in the morning. (never)
   _____
   4 Danny / be / at the library at night. (often)
   _____
   5 Nina / finish / work after 7:00 p.m. (usually)
   _____

COMMUNICATION PRACTICE

4C Student B

1 Read Ella's profile. Listen to Student A and answer his/her questions.

A *Where does Ella live?*   B *She lives in Philadelphia.*

Ella

Hi, I'm Ella. I live in Philadelphia. I'm a teacher at a school downtown. I usually get up at 6:00 a.m. I start work at 8:30, and I finish at 5:00 p.m. I love my job because I like children. To relax in the evening, I watch TV with my family. On the weekend, I play a lot of sports.

2 Ask Student A questions about Zain. Write his/her answers.

Zain

Questions

Where / live?
What / do?
Where / work?
What time / get up?
What time / finish work?
Why / like his job?
How / relax in the evening?
What / do on the weekend?

4D Student B

1 You are a salesclerk. Serve Student A. Remember to be polite.

A *Good morning. Can I have a cheese sandwich, please?*
B *Here you are.*
A *Thank you. How much is it?*
B *$1.99. Anything else?*

```
1 sandwich (cheese)   $1.99
6 eggs                $2.50
orange juice          $1.80
coffee                $3.29
pasta                 $1.50
Total                $11.08
```

2 You are a customer. Ask Student A for the things on your shopping list. Then ask how much each thing is. Remember to be polite.

```
Shopping list
2 bottles of water
some fish
1 four-cheese pizza
1 box of salad
1 chocolate cake
Total price = ?
```

5A Student B

1 Answer Student A's questions about Hana. You can only say *Yes, she can* or *No, she can't*.

A *Can she drive?*
B *Yes, she can.*

She can drive, speak Spanish, and play the guitar.
She can't cook Chinese food or dance salsa.

2 Look at the chart. Ask questions with *can* to guess which person Student A has.

	Sergio	Tom	Mark	Andy	Pete	Dennis
Can / take care of children?	✓	✗	✗	✗	✓	✗
Can / swim well?	✗	✓	✓	✗	✓	✓
Can / play the piano?	✗	✗	✗	✗	✓	✗
Can / speak French?	✓	✓	✗	✓	✗	✗
Can / write computer programs?	✗	✗	✓	✗	✓	✗

COMMUNICATION PRACTICE

5C Student B

1. Look at the profiles for a website called *New Friends*. Ask and answer questions with Student A to complete the information.

   B *What does Miguel think about cleaning?*   **A** *He doesn't like it.*

   ☺☺ = love, ☺ = like, ☹ = not like, ☹☹ = hate

   Daniela
☺	cooking
☺☺	cats and dogs
☹	early mornings

   Bill
☹	hiking
☹☹	housework
☺	books

   Monica
☹	going out
☹	bike riding
☺	movies

   Miguel
   - cleaning
   - reading
   - sports

   Claudio
   - swimming
   - watching movies
   - dancing

   Lucy
   - sleeping
   - animals
   - food and drink

2. Look at the profiles again. Find the best new friend for each person.

6A Student B

Look at the picture. Ask and answer questions with Student A to find six differences.

B *Are there any hotels?*
A *Yes, there are. There's one hotel.*
B *In my picture, there are two hotels.*
A *Is there a movie theater?*

6C Student B

1. Listen to Student A and draw the room.

   A *There's a bed. Next to the bed, there's a small table.*

   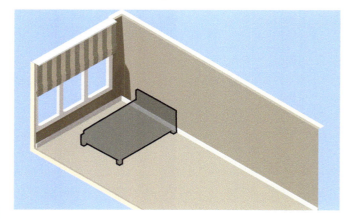

2. Describe your picture to Student A. He/She will draw it.

   B *There's a sofa in front of the window.*

COMMUNICATION PRACTICE

6D Student B

1 Listen to Student A. Look at the map and give directions.

A *Excuse me, is there a post office near here?*
B *Yes, there is. You go down Market Street …*
A *Could you repeat that, please?*

2 Ask Student A for directions to the places in the box. Listen and mark on the map where they are. Check the information if you need to.

> restaurant
> tourist information office
> grocery store

7A Student B

1 Answer Student A's questions about the famous people. You can only say *Yes, he/she was* or *No, he/she wasn't*.

A *Was Federico Fellini an artist?*
B *No, he wasn't.*
1 Federico Fellini was a movie director from Italy.
2 Janis Joplin was a singer from the U.S.
3 Nelson Mandela was a politician from South Africa.
4 Greta Garbo was an actor from Sweden.
5 Katsushika Hokusai was an artist from Japan.
6 Gabriel García Márquez was a writer from Colombia.

2 Ask Student A questions with *was* to match the famous people with their jobs and where they were from.

1	Frida Kahlo	soccer player	India
2	Johan Cruyff	musician	Spain
3	Celia Cruz	politician	Mexico
4	Jane Austen	singer	the Netherlands
5	Paco de Lucía	writer	Cuba
6	Jawaharlal Nehru	artist	the UK

7C Student B

1 Listen to Student A's questions. Correct the information.

A *Did Luke visit his grandparents last week?*
B *No, he didn't. He visited his grandparents last month.*
1 Luke visited his grandparents last month.
2 Kenny traveled to Brazil six years ago.
3 Clara played basketball yesterday.
4 Debbie cooked rice last night.
5 Steve worked as a teacher in the 1970s.
6 Amelia watched a movie yesterday morning.

2 Ask Student A questions. Find one incorrect piece of information for each person.

1 Zoe / stay / at a hotel near the beach / last year
2 Jim / study / German in college / in the 1990s
3 Antonia / walk / 18 miles / two days ago
4 Leandro / watch / a soccer game / last week
5 Rachel / start / a new job in Paris / last month
6 Tom / finish / work / half an hour ago

9C Questionnaire results

Mostly as: You don't like shopping, and you hate shopping malls. You prefer to spend money on other things. What do you do and how often do you do it?

Mostly bs: You like shopping, but you also like doing other things. A shopping mall is a good place to meet friends. How often do you go there?

Mostly cs: You love shopping – it's your life. You go shopping two or three times a week, and you shop online almost every day … but do you really need to buy all those things?

147

COMMUNICATION PRACTICE

8A Student B

1 Read the information and answer Student A's questions about what Lola did yesterday.

A *Where did Lola go?*   B *She went to her dad's birthday party.*

2 Ask Student A questions to find out what Mateo did yesterday.

Lola

She / go / her dad's birthday party
She / leave / the house at 7:00 p.m.
She / take / the train
She / wear / a new dress
She / buy / a book
She / have / a good time
She / sleep / on her dad's sofa

Mateo

Where / he / go?
he / go / by train?
he / take / a taxi to the airport?
What time / his flight / leave?
he / go / with friends?
he / sleep / on the plane?
he / have / a good trip?

8C Student B

1 Give Student A one minute to look at his/her picture. Ask him/her questions with *Was/Were there a/an/any ...?* and the words in the box. If he/she answers *Yes, there were*, ask *How many were there?*

| people | clouds | forest | trees |
| bus | houses | cars | river |

B *Were there any people?*   A *Yes, there were.*
B *How many were there?*   A *There were four people.*

2 Look at the picture for one minute. Then close your book and answer Student A's questions.

8D Student B

1 Read the situation in the box, and then look at the flowchart. You are the patient. Call Student A and have the conversation.

A *Hello, Green Lane Medical Center. Jorge speaking. How can I help you?*
B *Hello, my name's Anna Lopez. I'd like to see the doctor.*

> You don't feel well and want to see the doctor. Your head hurts. Your phone number is 951-742-5061.

Receptionist

Answer the phone. Give the name of the medical center/sports center and your name.

Ask more detailed questions.

Ask for the caller's contact details.

Finish the call.

Patient/Customer

Introduce yourself and say why you are calling.

Answer.

Answer.

2 Read the situation in the box, and then look at the flowchart again. You are the receptionist. Student A calls you. Have the conversation.

> You work at a sports center called The Fitness Factory. Answer the phone. Ask the person what sports they want to play.

COMMUNICATION PRACTICE

9A Student B

Look at the picture. Describe James, Grace, and Kara to Student A. Try to find six differences.

B *Grace is wearing a red dress and boots.*
A *In my picture, she's wearing shoes.*

9C Student B

Ask and answer the question *How often do/does ...?* with Student A to complete the chart.

B *How often does Laura have dinner in a restaurant?*
A *She has dinner in a restaurant twice a month.*

Laura	have dinner in a restaurant	
Jon and Andy	go to the movies	three or four times a year
Carlota	shop online	
Ahmed	ride a motorcycle	every day
Hope and Sara	check their e-mails	
Igor	read a new book	four or five times a year
Luisa and Raul	go swimming	
Yannis	go on vacation	once a year

10A Student B

Look at your schedule. Try to find a time when you can meet Student A. Ask and answer the question *What are you doing on ...?* for the different days.

A *What are you doing on Monday morning?*
B *I'm going to the gym. What about Monday afternoon?*

	Monday	Tuesday	Wednesday	Thursday	Friday
Morning	go to the gym	meet Simon for coffee		take bus to city	see dentist
Afternoon				visit art gallery	
Evening		go to a concert		stay at hotel	

149

COMMUNICATION PRACTICE

9A Student A

Look at the picture. Describe Aziz, Oscar, and Petra to Student B. Try to find six differences.

A *Aziz is looking at a white hat.*
B *In my picture, he's looking at some sunglasses.*

10C Student B

Ask Student A questions about his/her hobby in the correct tense. Write down his/her answers. Then guess what the hobby is.

B *How often do you do your hobby?*
A *I do it every weekend.*

Student A's hobby

Your hobby: basketball

1 How often / you / do / your hobby?		Twice a week.
2 When / you / start?		Last year.
3 it / be / expensive?		No, it's not.
4 it / be / dangerous?		No, it's not.
5 you / play / it in a team?		Yes, I do.
6 How many people / be there / in your team?		12 (but only five play at the same time).
7 Where / you / do / your hobby?		At the sports center.
8 you / do / your hobby next weekend?		Yes, we're going to Los Angeles for a game.

10D Students A and B

1 Complete the sentences. You can use real information or invent it.

About me
In my free time, I often _____ .
My favorite type of music is _____ .
Last weekend
I went shopping on Saturday, and I bought _____ .
Last weekend, I _____ .

My vacations
Last summer, I went to _____ .
When I'm on vacation, I usually _____ .
My plans
Next weekend, I'm meeting _____ .
For my next vacation, I'm _____ .

2 Read your sentences in pairs. Respond with interest using the words in the box.

| Oh really? | That's interesting. | That sounds good. | Wow, that's awesome! | Cool! | Great! |

A *In my free time, I often go skiing in the mountains.*
B *Wow, that's awesome!*

Irregular verbs

Infinitive	Simple past
be	was, were
become	became
begin	began
break	broke
bring	brought
buy	bought
choose	chose
come	came
cost	cost
do	did
drink	drank
drive	drove
eat	ate
fall	fell
feel	felt
find	found
fly	flew
get	got
give	gave
go	went
have	had
hear	heard
hold	held
hurt	hurt
keep	kept
know	knew

Infinitive	Simple past
leave	left
lose	lost
make	made
meet	met
pay	paid
put	put
read (/riːd/)	read (/red/)
ride	rode
run	ran
say	said
see	saw
sell	sold
sit	sat
sleep	slept
spend	spent
speak	spoke
stand	stood
swim	swam
take	took
teach	taught
tell	told
think	thought
understand	understood
wake	woke
wear	wore
win	won
write	wrote

58 St Aldates
Oxford
OX1 1ST
United Kingdom

ISBN: 978-84-668-2857-4
Tenth reprint: 2024

© Richmond / Santillana Global S.L. 2018

All rights reserved. No part of this book may be reproduced, stored in a retrieval system or transmitted in any form by any means, electronic, mechanical, photocopying, recording or otherwise, without the prior permission in writing of the Publisher.

Publishing Director: Deborah Tricker
Publisher: Simone Foster
Media Publisher: Sue Ashcroft
Content Developer: David Cole-Powney
Editors: Sue Jones, Debra Emmett, Tom Hadland, Fiona Hunt
Proofreaders: Pippa Mayfield, Shannon Neill, Jamie Bowman
Design Manager: Lorna Heaslip
Cover Design: This Ain't Rock'n'Roll, London
Design & Layout: Lorna Heaslip, emc design.
Photo Researcher: Magdalena Mayo
Learning Curve **video:** Mannic Media
Audio production: Tom, Dick and Debbie
App development: The Distance

We would also like to thank the following people for their valuable contribution to writing and developing the material:
Pamela Vittorio (Video Script Writer), Belen Fernandez (App Project Manager), Eleanor Clements (App Content Creator)

We would like to thank all those who have given their kind permission to reproduce material for this book:

Illustrators:
Simon Clare; Guillaume Gennet c/o Lemonade; John Goodwin; Sean Longcroft c/o KJA Artists; The Boy Fitzhammond c/o NB Illustration Ltd.

Photos:
J. Escandell.com; J. Jaime; J. Lucas; S. Enríquez; 123RF; ALAMY/ GerryRousseau, Jim Corwin, Moviestore collection Ltd, Simon Reddy, Stephen French, IanDagnall Computing, Joern Sackermann, dpa picture alliance, Serhii Kucher, ZUMA Press, Inc., All Canada Photos, London Entertainment, Everett Collection Inc, imageBROKER, Pongpun Ampawa, Peter Noyce GBR, Ian Allenden, AF archive, Elizabeth Livermore, Lex Rayton, Ted Foxx, Alvey & Towers Picture Library, Elizabeth Wake, Kristoffer Tripplaar, Lucas Vallecillos, Joe Fairs, Dinodia Photos, Peter D Noyce, Brigette Supernova, Pictorial Press Ltd, Collection Christophel, Jonathan Goldberg, Paul Hastie, Tierfotoagentur, REUTERS, Viktor Fischer, Art of Food, Andrey Armyagov, Alex Ramsay, Blend Images, B Christopher, Judith Collins, David Cabrera Navarro, Roman Tiraspolsky, robertharding, Michael Neelon(misc), Fredrick Kippe, Oleksiy Maksymenko Photography, Patti McConville, D. Callcut, Matthew Taylor, Rafael Angel Irusta Machin, Igor Kovalchuk, Mallorcaimages, Paul Quayle, Jozef Polc, Mick Sinclair, Michael Willis, Hugh Threlfall, ITAR-TASS Photo Agency, Bailey-Cooper Photography, jeremy sutton-hibbert, creativep, James Jeffrey Taylor, Oleksiy Maksymenko, Paul Smith, David Levenson, United Archives GmbH, Justin Kase zsixz, Simon Dack, Jeremy Pembrey, Barry Diomede, Alex Linch, Tomas Abad, Valentin Luggen, Sergey Soldatov, Iakov Filimonov, Anton Gvozdikov, Alex Segre, MBI, Paul Gibson, Stocksolutions, MEDIUM FORMAT COLLECTION/Balan Madhavan, allesalltag, David Robertson, Dmytro Zinkevych, Simon Dack News, Vaidas Bucys; CATERS NEWS AGENCY; FOCOLTONE; GETTY IMAGES SALES SPAIN/bjdlzx, Yuri_Arcurs, Reenya, Nikada, Paul Almasy, Martin Rose, Maskot, Lars Baron, JamieB, Annie Engel, Fosin2, Darumo, BraunS, artisticco, ajr_images, Bison_, AzmanL, artursfoto, pringletta, Dobino, Berezka_Klo, Indeed, Hero Images, KingWu, Tom Merton, NI QIN, Sam Edwards, Portra, ajaykampani, bgblue, leungchopan, c_kawi, s-c-s, kali9, SensorSpot, LeoPatrizi, Talaj, Pix11, Neyya, Dan Dalton, Chimpinski, DKart, shank_ali, Chris Ryan, londoneye, kickstand, kiankhoon, joto, Fuse, skynesher, asbe, gavran333, Zinkevych, KJA, AFP, ViewStock, John Lund/Sam Diephuis, Hiya Images/Corbis/ VCG, Tom Dulat, vm, imaginima, TF-Images, Ben Pipe Photography, Ridofranz, PPcavalry, Edda Dupree / EyeEm, Dave Hogan/MTV 2016, Lightcome, Isovector, VikramRaghuvanshi, FaraFaran, Cimmerian, Bet_ Noire, David C Tomlinson, Dave & Les Jacobs, unaemlag, technotr, Zoran Kolundzija, tarras79, stockcam, MacLife Magazine, Jetta Productions, Maya Karkalicheva, DGLimages, innovatedcaptures, FatCamera, Power Sport Images, Jasmina81, Lorraine Boogich, Mirrorpix, Kevin C. Cox - FIFA, Purestock, Caiaimage/Tom Merton, Stockbyte, Jason England / EyeEm, Ted Soqui, scyther5, Steven Swinnen / EyeEm, Weedezign, Westend61, Dave and Les Jacobs/Kolostock, chachamal, Cultura RM Exclusive/Frank and Helena, Echo, imagotres, julief514, karandaev, kpalimski, demaerre, Danny Martindale, Art-Y, omda_info, colematt, clubfoto, Allan Tannenbaum, DNY59, stevecoleimages, David Lees, DonNichols, JB Lacroix, asiseeit, Tuutikka, Tarzhanova, Thinkstock, Vladimir Godnik, Uwe Krejci, Venturelli, VladTeodor, Synergee, NurPhoto, Samuel de Roman, nycshooter, RuslanDashinsky, sorincolac, AndreyPopov, AngiePhotos, MistikaS, JGalione, Choreograph, Fotoplanner, Leah Puttkammer, Hero images, John Keeble, Liam Norris, JANIFEST, LWA/Dann Tardif, Ron Galella, Rose_Carson, IvanMiladinovic, Shana Novak, Simon Sarin, T3 Magazine, Floortje, Hung_ Chung_Chih, artlensfoto, domin_domin, Frank van Delft, macrovector, michaeljung, penguenstok, Flashpop, DenisKot, Wavebreakmedia, Creative, Claudiad, Sheikoevgeniya, Philipp Nemenz, Bettmann, Al Freni, EmirMemedovski, wir0man, pshonka, Anthony Harvey, Anadolu Agency, mrak_hr, mixetto, i love images, mbbirdy, kivoart, SnegiriBureau, Rick Friedman, jsnover, iconeer, Monty Rakusen, gilaxia, Maksim Ozerov, gerenme, MStudioImages, MATJAZ SLANIC, andresr, Jupiterimages, Jon Feingersh, adekvat, Jamie Garbutt, Jack Mitchell, Mark Cuthbert, R-O-M-A, Paras Griffin, Peathegee Inc, Radius Images, Gabriel Rossi, FrozenShutter, blueringmedia, davidcreacion, NuStock, justhavealook, reportman1985, zeljkosantrac, Dougal Waters, David Redfern, Askold Romanov, Digital Vision, Krasyuk, Javier Pierini, Marc Romanelli, Neustockimages, Andersen Ross, Alistair Berg, Steven Puetzer, Todor Tsvetkov, Devonyu, franckreporter, Anthony Charles, Danita Delimont, senkoumelnik, ferrantraite, Chesnot, ersinkisacik, bluejayphoto, NicolasMcComber, Photos.com Plus, Robyn Mackenzie, Astarot, Tony Vaccaro, Santiago Felipe, Tristan Fewings, Tetra Images, dogayusufdokdok, nicoletaionescu, praetorianphoto, vgajic, Sofie Delauw, Birgit R / EyeEm, Christopher Polk, PeopleImages, Henn Photography, KavalenkavaVolha, Kittisak_Taramas, tunart, Mike Coppola, Nicolas McComber, Tatjana Kaufmann, LuisPortugal, christopherarndt, Adrian Weinbrecht, Chris Sattlberger, subjug, JuliarStudio, Juice Images, Jrg Mikus / EyeEm, sturti, Roberto Westbrook, Tanya Constantine, Valery Sharifulin, Jason Hawkes, Image Source, IMAGEMORE Co, Ltd., Jacob Wackerhausen, seb_ra, crossroadscreative, m-imagephotography, DEA PICTURE LIBRARY, Hiroyuki Ito, Erik Isakson, EvgeniyaTiplyashina, Hill Street Studios, lushik, Mondadori Portfolio, Andreas Hein / EyeEm, Axelle/ Bauer-Griffin, Emad Aljumah, Deborah Kolb, monkeybusinessimages, Alexandr Sherstobitov, laflor, Michael Ochs Archives, Science Photo Library, BJI / Blue Jean Images, Dan MacMedan, ChrisHepburn, kzenon, Banar Fil Ardhi / EyeEm, PhotoAlto/Sigrid Olsson, Jade Albert Studio, Inc.. New York Daily News Archive, Constantinos Kollias / EyeEm, Chris Wa.ter, Photo by Claude-Olivier Marti, Kelly Cheng Travel Photography, Blend Images - Jose Luis Pelaez Inc, shapecharge, Compassionate Eye Foundation/ Steven Errico, gbh007; HIGHRES PRESS STOCK/AbleStock.com; I. PREYSLER; ISTOCKPHOTO/ Getty Images Sales Spain; Devasahayam Chandra Dhas, Andreas Herpens, calvindexter, popovaphoto, Phazemedia, denphumi, SolStock, Pali Rao, JoeLena; J. M.ª BARRES; SHUTTERSTOCK/ Glenn Copus/Evening Standard, Olivia Rutherford, MARIUS ALEXANDER, Iakov Filimonov, Sergey Novikov, Blend Images, terekhov igor; Farmer's Daughter; Jono Williams; Andrew Hyde; Aimee Giese; Museum of London; Samsung; SERIDEC PHOTOIMAGENES CD; Telegraph Media Group Limited; ARCHIVO SANTILLANA

Cover Photo: GETTY IMAGES SALES SPAIN/mixetto

We would like to thank the following reviewers for their valuable feedback which has made Personal Best possible. We extend our thanks to the many teachers and students not mentioned here.
Brad Bawtinheimer, Manuel Hidalgo, Paulo Dantas, Diana Bermúdez, Laura Gutiérrez, Hardy Griffin, Ángi Conti, Christopher Morabito, Hande Kokce, Jorge Lobato, Aimee Giese, Leonardo Mercato, Mercilinda Ortiz, Wendy López

The Publisher has made every effort to trace the owner of copyrighted material; however, the Publisher will correct any involuntary omission at the earliest opportunity.

Printed in Brazil by Forma Certa
Lote. 800402